FORECASTING SALES AND PLANNING PROFITS

A NO-NONSENSE GUIDE FOR THE GROWING BUSINESS

FORECASTING SALES AND PLANNING PROFITS

A NO-NONSENSE GUIDE FOR THE GROWING BUSINESS

by

KENNETH E. MARINO
Associate Professor of Management
College of Business Administration
San Diego State University

Probus Publishing Company
Chicago, Illinois

Library of Congress Cataloging-in-Publication Data

Marino, Kenneth E.
    Forecasting sales and planning profits.

    Bibliography: p.
    Includes index.
    1. Sales forecasting.   I. Title.
HF5415.2.M318   1986   658.8'18   86-12243
ISBN 0-917253-50-7

Library of Congress Catalog Card No. 86-12243

Printed in the United States of America

1 2 3 4 5 6 7 8 9 0

To Barbara, Eric, and Cara

Contents

PREFACE... ix

ACKNOWLEDGEMENTS.. xi

CHAPTER 1: INTRODUCTION....................................... 1

CHAPTER 2: SALES FORECASTING IN
           GROWING FIRMS..................................... 5
Why Not Forecast Sales?... 8
Purposes and Benefits of Sales Forecasting.................. 11

CHAPTER 3: SALES FORECASTING TECHNIQUES...... 19
Data-Based Techniques.. 21
Judgmental Techniques... 22
Market Potential–Sales Requirements Method.............. 23
Case Study 3-1: EMC Site Expansion......................... 26

CHAPTER 4: DEFINING THE TARGET MARKET.......... 39
Retail Markets.. 43
Industrial Markets... 44

CHAPTER 5: ESTIMATING MARKET POTENTIAL........ 49
Trade Area Definition... 51
Case Study 5-1: The Locker Room............................. 56
Determining Market Potential................................... 58
Case Study 5-2: The Floral Supply............................ 65
Case Study 5-3: WXXX-FM...................................... 69

CHAPTER 6: DERIVING SALES REQUIREMENTS......... 73
Estimating Start-up Expenses..................................... 76
Estimating Operating Expenses................................... 78
Data Sources... 83
Constructing Sales Budgets.. 85
Case Study 6-1: The Dark Room................................. 87

CHAPTER 7: DEVELOPING A REALISTIC
               FORECAST... 97
Initial Comparisons... 99
Judging Likely Sales Growth..................................... 101
Preparing the Forecasts.. 105
Case Study 7-1: The Dark Room (continued)............... 106

CHAPTER 8: SALES FORECASTING AS A
               MANAGEMENT CONTROL TOOL.......... 115
Management Control.. 117
Case Study 8-1: The Floral Supply (continued)........... 122
Using a Continuous Forecast..................................... 124

APPENDIX A: Secondary Data Sources....................... 127

APPENDIX B: Some Selected Readings for
                Extension and Future Development....... 137

APPENDIX C: Personal Computer
                Spreadsheet Packages.......................... 141

APPENDIX D: Sales Forecasting Techniques............... 147

GLOSSARY... 161

INDEX... 173

Preface

As any experienced businessperson knows, forecasting sales and revenues is an inexact science at best. Even in large companies with sophisticated computer systems and experienced statisticians, the process is difficult and uncertain. Markets and market conditions change, making interpolations from historical data useless. Even more difficult, what does a company do when it attempts to project sales and revenues on new ventures?

If it is difficult for large companies to forecast effectively, imagine the problem faced by medium-sized and growing businesses without benefit of high-priced talent and systems. This book was written to help with this very problem. Companies *can* develop a system for forecasting sales and revenues that is cost-effective and reliable.

Many companies dismiss forecasting sales and revenues because it is inexact. To my way of thinking, this is a mistake, and a serious one at that. Forecasting forces a business discipline onto management that would not normally be there without it. Forecasting will help management understand and control costs and unnecessary expenses. Further, it will ensure careful inventory control.

In order to make forecasting as simple as possible, I recommend the *market potential/sales requirement* method of sales and revenue forecasting. This method approaches the forecasting problem from two perspectives. The market potential approach estimates the total market volume in dollars or units in a particular trade area. The sales requirement approach estimates the volume necessary for the business to meet various performance targets. The two approaches together combine the best of "top-down" and "bottom-up" forecasting.

This book will explain and illustrate the steps involved in forecasting sales and revenues using this combined method. Real companies, from a variety of industries, have been chosen to show the process in real situations.

Kenneth E. Marino

Acknowledgements

The experiences of a number of small business owners and prospective owners are reflected in this book. Their plans, problems, and questions were instrumental in defining the content and organization of the text. While they are too numerous to name, the opportunity to discuss their ventures with them is gratefully acknowledged.

Discussions with colleagues at the University of Kentucky and elsewhere have also contributed to this effort. In particular, I'd like to thank Marc Dollinger at UK, and Rick Castaldi and Alex De Noble at San Diego State. The support of the College of Business and Economics at The University of Kentucky is also acknowledged.

Bob Sehlinger, managing editor of Menasha Ridge Press, originally approached me with the idea for this book, and has offered suggestions and encouragement along the way. Becky Sanders typed the manuscript several times, and did her usual outstanding job.

Chapter 1

Introduction

This book is intended for owners and operators of growing businesses. The focus is on forecasting sales under conditions of uncertainty, but this is really a book on planning. While a sales forecast is, in and of itself, a plan, its existence guides decisions about supplies, money, manpower and so on in the future. Of course, making decisions about the future is what planning is all about.

The book differs from other treatments of forecasting in three ways. First, the focus is on growing firms and the problems inherent in understanding local markets. Second, the emphasis is on general management skills and reasoned judgment as opposed to statistical extrapolations. Third, the forecasting approach relies on how to acquire and use data gathered and published by government agencies and trade associations rather than on the collection and analysis of primary market data.

The development of a sales forecast requires the integration of data and judgments drawn from various sources. The general framework advocated here for preparing a forecast has been labeled the *market potential–sales requirements* method.

After a discussion of the benefits of forecasting in Chapter 2, the MP-SR method is introduced and illustrated in Chapter 3. In Chapters 4 through 7, the method is broken into its main components and each group of tasks is discussed in detail and illustrated through case studies of actual retail and service businesses. In the final chapter the use of a forecast to monitor and control the operation of the firm is explored.

Four appendices are included as a service to the reader. The first is a guide to published data sources. These sources offer valuable information at nominal fees. The second appendix is a selected bibliography of texts available to continue your development as a forecaster. Topics include statistical forecasting techniques and marketing research. The third appendix is a bibliography of software and tutorial guides to the use of a personal computer in business forecasting. The final appendix is a description of other sales forecasting techniques.

The discussions and illustrations have been designed to impart specific skills to the reader. By the end of this book, you will be able to

- Develop a profile of your target customers
- Use census and other data to estimate the market potential of your trading area
- Estimate the capital requirements and operating expenses of your business
- Determine the budgeted sales level required to support your business or profit center
- Formulate a realistic monthly sales forecast
- Use your forecast to direct resources and control your business

The prerequisites for employing the forecasting process are few. A rudimentary knowledge of accounting and finance concepts is presumed, but the major prerequisite is the ability to think realistically about the behavior of customers and competitors.

Chapter 2

Sales Forecasting in Growing Firms

Accurate sales forecasts are essential for management planning and control in virtually all business firms. The sales forecast is usually the first step in a planning process and, when formulated, it triggers a variety of other decisions. For instance, decisions on production volume, raw materials procurement, staffing, and cash budgeting are all formulated with a forecasted level of sales activity in mind.

Several studies conducted among members of the Fortune 500 indicate widespread use of sales forecasting techniques of one kind or another. While comparable data on sales forecasting in smaller firms is not available, the use of any sort of formal sales forecasting procedure in growing businesses and even in profit centers of large corporations is believed to be the exception rather than the rule. Unfortunately, the benefits that accrue to a firm operating with forecasted sales levels are just as important to small firms and profit centers as they are to larger business firms.

WHY NOT FORECAST SALES?

In discussions with business owners, managers of profit centers, and business specialists such as accountants, lawyers, and SBA bankers, four reasons were offered to explain why many firms don't prepare sales forecasts:

- Lack of data
- Lack of time
- Lack of expertise
- Lack of accuracy

Lack of Data

Many sales forecasting techniques require data that are generally either not available or far too costly for a growing business or profit center to justify. The capacity of a large firm to spread the cost of market research over much larger unit volumes is a distinct advantage. Also, historical data on industry sales activity and correlates of sales activity, such as disposable personal income, may be available for national or regional geographic markets served by large firms, but not for local markets served by a small retail or wholesale operation. The solution to this very real problem is the resourceful use of published data sources.

Government publications such as those from the Department of Commerce are particularly relevant to sales forecasting, and they are available for nominal fees. Trade associations can also provide a wealth of information on the businesses they represent—usually for free.

In Chapter 5 a variety of published data sources are discussed, and their use illustrated. While the lack of data can be a serious problem to the business forecaster, the fact is there are very few products so revolutionary and few markets so unknown that we can't find some sort of useful secondary data.

Lack of Time

The firm owner or manager wears a number of different hats involving contact with employees, vendors, financial institutions, and customers. Further, as the chief executive they are drawn into the solution of virtually every operating problem and policy issue. It is not surprising then to hear legions of business operators claim they don't have time to plan and develop sales forecasts. However, if we recognize planning as a critical management function—one that affects the prosperity and survival of the firm—time must be set aside for planning and forecasting activities.

Owners or managers who can't find the time to plan either have to redefine their own work activities or consciously set aside a block of time, perhaps outside of normal business hours, to devote to planning. Delegation of authority to make certain operating decisions can serve to both develop management talent that may be necessary for future growth and to free up the time of the owner. Recurring decisions, such as production scheduling or entry-level hiring decisions, are good candidates for delegation. Scheduling planning sessions on Saturday mornings, when day-to-day interruptions can be avoided, has worked well in many firms.

Lack of time is a well-worn excuse that is no more valid here than it is in most other situations where it's evoked. The fact is, a manager who can't find time to plan is already demonstrating what an ineffective manager he or she is. Make the time.

Lack of Expertise

As we'll see in the next chapter, on sales forecasting techniques, there are some very sophisticated approaches to forecasting. Some techniques presume substantial statistical training and computer capabilities. As with the data issue we've already discussed, large firms have the unit volume to justify the overhead expense of a corporate staff with the necessary skills.

However, there are also forecasting techniques that emphasize general management skills as opposed to specialist skills. The approach to sales forecasting presented in this book relies on the common sense and business judgment that a successful manager or business operator should possess. That judgment coupled with market and cost data from published sources and an objective view of target markets, products, and competitors can lead to reasoned sales forecasts.

So, while the lack of expertise is a valid excuse regarding some data-based forecasting techniques, there are other approaches to forecasting. By relying on what are defined in Chapter 3 as judgmental techniques, technical expertise is much less an issue.

Lack of Accuracy

The final excuse of business operators who don't forecast sales is the most frequently heard: that they can't forecast accurately enough to be useful. Managers that evaluate a previous sales forecasting effort by how closely it predicted actual end-of-year sales often lament "We're so far off every year, I don't know why we bother to forecast in the first place." Such an attitude ignores some of the major benefits associated with preparing a forecast. Of course, accuracy is desirable in forecasting situations, but it may not always be achievable.

The environments in which many firms operate are not stable enough to permit high degrees of forecast accuracy. There are a number of reasons for this. The most important are below:

- **Rapidly changing customer preferences** that can create volatile shifts in demand, particularly when serving retail markets.

- **Few entry barriers** to block the start-up of new competitors. Entry of new competitors is associated with the increased use of competitive tactics such as price discounts and promotions.
- **Fluctuating input costs** that affect all businesses; but many firms lack the ability to negotiate volume adjustments with materials suppliers and interest costs with financial institutions.

In addition to these factors that influence sales volume, the most fundamental approach to stabilizing revenues followed by large firms is diversification. However, due to resource constraints, most growing firms pursue concentration strategies. The addition of a complementary business tends to reduce fluctuation in sales and, therefore, the riskiness of the concern. Combinations of real estate brokerage with insurance sales and heating with air conditioning service are obvious diversification moves.

Overall, we must recognize that forecast accuracy is a desirable but not always attainable goal. All forecasts are based on assumptions about the economy, competitor behavior, interest rates, and consumer demand, to name only a few. The factors mentioned above influence the validity of the assumptions on which the forecast is based, and subsequently its accuracy. If we recognize that forecasts are by their very nature always "wrong" to some extent, we can turn our attention to the other benefits that accrue from a forecasting effort.

PURPOSES AND BENEFITS OF SALES FORECASTING

Sales forecasts are necessary in several types of business decisions. New ventures, product line additions, and geographic expansion via new site locations are fairly common business decisions that require sales estimates. Once prepared, forecasts can serve multiple purposes within the same organization.

Purposes of Sales Forecasting

Consider the following illustrations of forecasting situations.

ISI Industrial Supply, Inc. (ISI), is engaged in the distribution of maintenance and safety supplies to the mining and construction industries. The founder, John Mean, had established the firm after several years' experience as a field salesperson with an established distributor of similar lines. ISI has distributor relationships with respected manufacturers of safety glasses, pressure gauges, hose and worm gear clamps, and several lines of rubber hosing for fluid transfer applications. While presently profitable, Mr. Means feels he is losing sales by not offering a line of hydraulic hoses. His existing clients operate mining machines and earth-moving equipment that routinely require hydraulic line replacements. A major supplier of rubber products is considering ISI as a hydraulic line distributor but is concerned about ISI's potential sales volume.

Offering this new product line will require the purchase of several pieces of new equipment for cutting and crimping fittings to the hoses. In addition, an initial inventory of hose in various diameters (1/4''–2''), and connectors for each size is estimated to require a $300,000 investment. Mr. Means has a good banking relationship, but his banker needs some assurance that the sales revenue generated by this new product line justifies an equipment and working capital loan.

EMC Emergency Medical Center was founded by Dr. Anthony Petrillo as a free-standing emergency center (FEC). The FEC concept, which is relatively new to the health delivery system, is a cross between a physician's office and a hospital emergency room. The typical FEC offers extended hours (8 AM–11 PM), has lab and X-ray facilities, and will treat any non–life-threatening trauma or medical problem on a no-appointment basis.

The Emergency Medical Center opened in 1982 and had grown substantially during its first year. When Dr. Petrillo was informed that a good location in another section of the same city had become available, he considered opening a second office. From a study of traffic patterns and population density in the area, proximity to area hospitals, and the sales experience in EMC #1, sales forecasts for EMC #2 were prepared. After lease-hold improvements, equipment costs, and operating expenses were estimated, the decision was made to open EMC #2.

The facility was opened with a fanfare of advertising and press releases. Sales immediately exceeded the first month's forecast. After several months of continued growth, sales (i.e., patient visits) leveled off at a point below breakeven. Forecasted growth did not occur and cumulative operating losses were mounting. Remedial action, in the form of intensified media advertising, was taken. A personal selling program directed at business establishments was started in an effort to treat more work-related injuries. Neither effort stimulated the necessary sales growth. Less than one year after opening, EMC #2 was determined to be a failure and operations were consolidated with the original, and still successful, EMC #1.

Central Bearings and Drives, Inc. Central Bearings and Drives, Inc., is a distributor of sprockets, belts, rotors, seals, and replacement parts for industrial equipment. Corporate headquarters is responsible for procurement and provides administrative support for three branch stores dispersed across two states. Because the inventory is large (and some of its inventory items are quite expensive), and because the lead time for orders varies with each of its suppliers, sales forecasting is complex.

Forecasts are prepared for each major product line by each branch store manager. They are reviewed and aggregated at headquarters. The aggregated forecasts allow the headquarters purchasing agent to seek the most favorable terms and the transportation manager to direct shipments to the branch stores. Deviations from forecasts are helpful in redeploying inventory to branch sites experiencing unexpected demand.

Forecast accuracy is also a component in the annual performance evaluations of branch managers.

Benefits of Sales Forecasting

In each of these illustrations the sales forecast serves a slightly
different purpose. The forecast is a central component of a
broader business planning activity. As such, the forecast offers
several benefits to the business manager. A realistic sales
forecast

- Stimulates planning
- Facilitates communication with outsiders
- Promotes coordination within the firm, and
- Supports management control activities

These benefits accrue to a firm due to the *existence* of a forecast. Before the benefits are discussed, it should be recognized
that less tangible, but equally important, benefits result from
the *process* of forecasting. As we'll see, preparing a forecast
requires a manager to specify and think in detailed terms about

a) Target market groups and customer segments to be served
b) Competitors, both existing and potential, and
c) Assumptions about the local economy, its growth and
   prosperity

In other words, the process of forecasting forces us to take a
very thorough look at our business and our markets. The
insights and understanding gained from this process may well
be the most valuable benefit of forecasting.

Stimulating Planning   A sales forecast is a central component of an overall short-term operating plan. Indeed, without a forecasted level of sales activity it is virtually impossible
to make staffing, inventory, and financial decisions.

Figure 2-1 depicts the relationships among various plans
and the sales forecast.

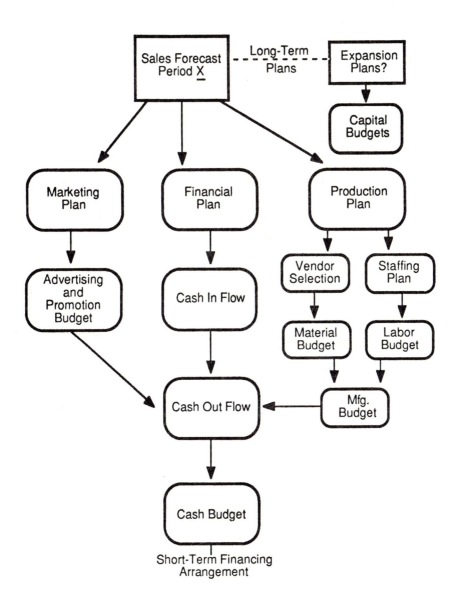

FIGURE 2-1 RELATIONSHIP OF THE SALES FORECAST
TO OTHER PLANNING ACTIVITIES

The supporting documents and budgets form the foundation for the effective management of operations. All too often these decisions are not thought through in a rigorous fashion because they're so *uncertain*; that is, "It all depends on what we can sell!" The sales forecast, even if we prepare it as a range (from pessimistic to optimistic sales levels), provides a reasonably sound starting point from which other decisions can be made.

Facilitating Communication Every business manager will occasionally need to communicate his or her business intentions to outsiders. These outsiders are generally financial institutions, but they could also be potential investors or suppliers. A realistic sales forecast details a number of aspects of a business that outsiders cannot be expected to be familiar with. The forecast represents common ground on which both the owner or manager and knowledgeable outsiders can assess the business. In addition, the sales forecast, the logic on which it was developed, and the assumptions on which it is based reflect on the business sense of the owners and managers. A forecast that is based on unsupported assumptions or that incorporates wildly optimistic growth projections indicates that current management is careless, unrealistic, or both. This may not be the firm an outsider would want to extend credit to, or enter a distributor relationship with.

Promoting Coordination A forecast is a target that, when communicated to the members of the firm, sets their expectations at a uniform level. This is particularly important in a firm that has grown to the point that its management team represents diverse functional areas or diverse geographic sites.

The forecast ensures that the marketing manager and the production supervisor each understand the expected activity level and can tailor their functional activities accordingly. The coordination illustrated in the Central Bearings and Drives example would be impossible in the absence of forecasts.

Supporting Management Control   Because the forecast is a target, it becomes a basis for determining success or failure. Evaluating performance at the end of the forecast period (quarter, year) is useful, but to continually evaluate progress toward forecasted activity levels on a weekly or monthly basis offers a more powerful management control device. The essence of management control is to institute corrective action *in a timely fashion.* Promotion budgets, purchasing plans, staffing plans, and capital investment plans can all be affected by deviations in forecasted sales levels.

In the next chapter basic forecasting techniques are reviewed and the market potential–sales requirements approach to forecasting advocated in this book is introduced.

Chapter 3

Sales Forecasting Techniques

There are a number of different approaches to forecasting sales. They fall into two categories: data-based techniques and judgmental techniques.*

DATA-BASED TECHNIQUES

Data-based forecasting techniques are objective and rely on historical data in the formulation of a forecast. The historical data required are usually (1) sales volume of the product or product line and (2) data on variables that influence sales—such as per capita income, the number of households in the trade area, or a measure of the health of the local economy (sales tax receipts or gross payroll, for example). In general, data-based techniques use historical data to develop a mathemati-

*The reader will also find a summary of major statistical methods of forecasting in Appendix D.

cal model that explains variation in historical sales figures as a function of changes in the other variables. Once the model (actually an equation) is estimated on the historical data, a sales forecast can be computed. For example, suppose the number of households in the trade area affects sales volume at the local supermarket. If the number of households is growing, the *future* number of households can be entered into the equation and an estimate of *future* supermarket volume can be computed. The techniques range in sophistication from simple correlation analysis to complex economic modeling involving systems of equations. All the techniques require some degree of statistical skill and assume that the past can be used to predict the future. A discussion of data-based techniques is beyond the scope and intent of this book. However, for the interested reader, a bibliography of practical and readable texts on the statistical approaches to forecasting is presented in Appendix B.

JUDGMENTAL TECHNIQUES

In situations where sales history is nonexistent, as with a new venture, or where sales history is irrelevant due to changing market conditions, judgmental techniques must be relied upon. These techniques, as a group, are distinguished from the data-based techniques in that they require less historical data and less statistical expertise. Each judgmental technique is a method for making an educated guess concerning future sales levels. Four of the six judgmental techniques listed in Figure 3-1 rely on estimates made by knowledgable individuals—executives, salespersons, or industry experts. Historical analogy involves formulating a forecast based on the history of a similar product or service in a similar market. Intention-to-buy surveys base future sales estimates on the stated purchase intentions of a sample of the target market population.

Judgmental	Data-Based
Sales Force Estimates	Correlation Analysis
Executive Consensus	Multiple Regression
Industry Expert Estimates	Time Series Analysis
Delphi Method	Input-Output Analysis
Historical Analogy	Econometric Models
Intention-to-Buy Survey	

FIGURE 3-1   TAXONOMY OF SALES FORECASTING TECHNIQUES*

The approach for developing a forecast advocated here is judgmental and may use elements of any of the judgmental techniques that have been mentioned. The *market potential–sales requirements* method approaches the forecast problem from two perspectives. The market potential approach estimates the total market volume in either dollars or units in a particular trade area. The sales requirement approach estimates the volume necessary for the business to meet various performance targets. The results of the two approaches are then combined to form a realistic forecast. This combination of what have been labeled "top-down" and "bottom-up" approaches is a fairly common forecasting method.

The balance of this book illustrates and explains the various steps involved in this dual approach to developing forecasts. Before we look at each step in detail, an overview of the method and an illustration are in order.

MARKET POTENTIAL–SALES REQUIREMENTS METHOD

The *market potential–sales requirements* method (MP-SR) reflects several beliefs regarding forecasting in growing firms. First, forecasting is not an exact science; hence, the dual

---

*Appendix D provides a summary of each of these forecasting methods.

approach just discussed. In other words, we prefer to develop a forecast from several different perspectives and then consider a consensus forecast. Second, the MP-SR method recognizes forecasting as a recursive process. That is, the final forecast is the result of several "rounds" of forecasting in which market areas are redefined or operating expenses are modified until a realistic forecast that represents acceptable performance is developed.

The MP-SR method is diagrammed in Figure 3-2. The "top-down" (market potential) and the "bottom-up" (sales requirements) approaches can be conducted simultaneously. In fact, they can be conducted by different individuals. The marketing or sales manager might prepare the market potential side of the forecast while accounting prepares the sales requirements estimate. In some firms, the outside experts might work with the owner on the sales requirements approach.

Combining these two estimates represents the real judgmental activity in the MP-SR method. At this step the number of competitors and their likely behavior must be assessed. Total market growth and sources of competitive advantage must also be considered during this step. The "revise?" question represents the recursive aspect of the method. If it is determined that the likely proportion of the total market is too small to support the business or meet the owner's objectives, we can attempt to revise the plans. Perhaps a redefinition of the target market is possible, although revisions on the sales requirements side are more common. For instance, cutting start-up and capital expenses, or reducing operating expenses through revised staffing plans or promotion budgets can lead to an acceptable revision of the forecast. In some situations, given the realities of the market and the cost structure of the firm, an acceptable forecast can not be reached. These are the ventures it is advisable to walk away from. To illustrate the MP-SR method, let's consider a situation faced by Dr. Petrillo of the Emergency Medical Center.

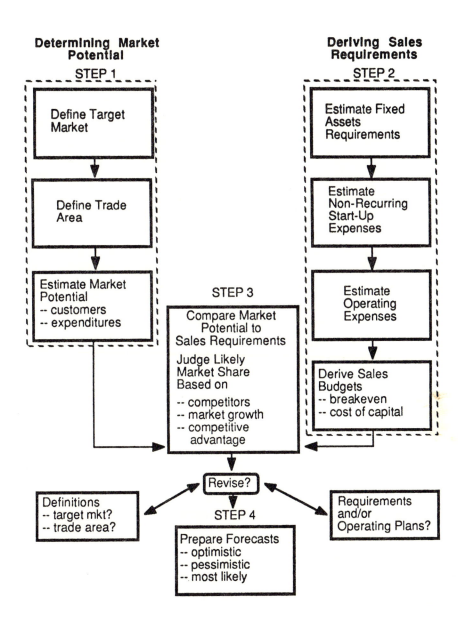

FIGURE 3-2   MARKET POTENTIAL–SALES REQUIREMENT
APPROACH TO SALES FORECASTING

Case Study 3-1—EMC Site Expansion

The Emergency Medical Center (EMC) described briefly in the last chapter had recovered from the ill-fated site expansion within their local trade area. Nonetheless, multiple sites offer important economic advantages in advertising, supply ordering, and management. Consequently, Dr. Petrillo continued to search out feasible locations for a second EMC facility.

A real estate developer has contacted Dr. Petrillo concerning a site being developed in a small town about twenty-two miles outside the headquarters city of EMC. The site is at the intersection of an Interstate and a state highway and offers excellent visibility. The town has one general hospital, a student health service on the campus of a university, and about eighteen private physicians' offices. The developer and several of his financial backers feel that the growth of the community has created the need for additional medical facilities. They've proposed the construction of a single-story building on the site and have offered to finish a 2000-square-foot section to Dr. Petrillo's specifications. A three-year lease with renewal options at an annual rental of $7.50/sq. ft. is available. Dr. Petrillo requires a sales forecast for the venture in order to make a decision regarding the expansion and, if the decision is positive, to negotiate with a bank and an equipment leasing firm.

Step 1. Determining Market Potential

Target Market The market for ambulatory health care includes the entire population. All people are subject to both minor injuries such as cuts, sprains, or fractures and to minor illnesses such as colds and flu.

Consultants to the industry and the National Association of Free-Standing Emergency Centers (NAFEC), the industry trade association, focus on a more narrowly defined target market. They report that the primary targets for EMC services are families with young children, working women, and individuals with no regular physician. While these refinements will be of value in designing and placing advertising messages, it is best to consider the total population as the target market for feasibility purposes.

Trade Area   The city is a small community. The proposed site can be reached in 10 to 12 minutes driving time from anywhere within the city limits. The site is on the opposite side of town from the general hospital. Virtually none of the population would have to drive past a competitor to reach the EMC site. Hence, the trade area is defined as the entire city.

Market Potential   The 1980 census of population reports that the city and immediate residential areas was the home of 27,531 people. The residents make up 8924 households. The town has enjoyed substantial growth over the decade of 1970–1980. The number of housing units grew 55 percent over the decade. This is a positive sign in that the people relocating to the area are less likely to have established physician relationships. Based on discussions with city officials and members of the Chamber of Commerce, growth is believed to have continued, but at a slower rate, during the 1980s.

In terms of market potential, NAFEC estimates that on the average, individuals experience between 1 and 2 incidents of minor trauma or illness per year. Based on assumed rates of population growth, estimates of total market potential in terms of patient visits can be developed.

Total patient visits for 1984 are estimated to be somewhere between 28,649 and 64,414. This is a rather broad interval; perhaps too broad to be of use. The middle column of Exhibit 3-2 represents a more reasonable interval. Based on an average incident rate of 1.5 per person-year, total market potential for the area would be estimated at 43,000 to 48,000 patient visits per year.

Numbers of People

	Annual Growth = 1% (pessimistic)	Annual Growth = 2.5% (likely)	Annual Growth = 4% (optimistic)
1980	27531	27531	27531
1981	27806	28219	28632
1982	28084	28925	29778
1983	28365	29648	30969
1984	28649	30389	32207
1985	28935	31149	33496
1986	29225	31928	34835
1987	29517	32726	36229

EXHIBIT 3-1   POPULATION PROJECTIONS
BASED ON VARIOUS GROWTH RATES

TOTAL 1984 PATIENT VISITS

Population Growth	Average Visits Per Person-Year		
	1	1.5	2.0
1.0% (pessimistic)	28649	42973	57298
2.5% (likely)	30389	45584	60778
4.0% (optimistic)	32207	48310	64414

EXHIBIT 3-2   LOGAN TOTAL PATIENT VISITS BASED ON
GROWTH AND ANNUAL INCIDENT ASSUMPTIONS

Step 2. Deriving Sales Requirements

Fixed Asset Requirements Fixed assets required for the site are entirely equipment costs. Leasehold improvements such as plumbing modifications and remodeling will be avoided due to the developer's new construction. The required equipment includes both medical equipment and standard office furniture and equipment.

Local medical supply and office supply dealers were the source of price estimates presented in Exhibits 3-3 and 3-4. These dealers are familiar with the used equipment markets in the area. Price estimates reflect a mix of new and used equipment. Total fixed asset requirements are estimated at $64,500.

Medical Equipment ($51,000)

Laboratory ($6000)
Refrigerator
Microscope
Blood gas analyzer
Autoclave
Stain tray
Urinometer
Centrifuge
Microcrit reader
Incubator

X-ray ($30,000)
X-ray system
Processor
Float table
Bucky table

General ($15,000)
Trauma stretchers
I.U. stands
EKG
Oxygen
Suction unit
Suture sets
Ambu bag
Wheelchair
Crash cart
Head lamp
Surgical table
Cast cutter
Defibrillator
Woods lamp
Laryngoscope

**EXHIBIT 3-3   MEDICAL EQUIPMENT REQUIREMENTS
FOR PROPOSED EMC FACILITY**

Office and Miscellaneous ($13,500)

Office Equipment ($3500)
Desks/chairs
File cabinets
Typewriter
Calculators
Desk-top copier

Misc. Furniture ($4000)
Breakroom furniture
Microwave/compact refrigerator
Waiting room furniture
Window treatments/fixtures

Exterior Signs ($6000)
Free-standing illuminated sign
Building-mounted signs

EXHIBIT 3-4   OFFICE AND MISCELLANEOUS FURNITURE AND EQUIPMENT REQUIREMENTS FOR PROPOSED EMC FACILITY

Nonrecurring Start-up Expenses One-time expenses involved in opening an EMC-type facility are substantial. Exhibit 3-5 presents these estimated preopening expenses. The figures were compiled from Dr. Petrillo's earlier experience with EMC #1.

Direct mail advertising (preopening)	2,300
Legal/accounting	300
Rent/utilities deposits	4,226
Prepaid malpractice insurance	3,100
Housekeeping/security services	500
Initial medical supplies inventory	3,803
Nonphysician salaries (preopening)	1,500
Sundry	2,000
	$17,729

EXHIBIT 3-5   NONRECURRING START-UP EXPENSES FOR PROPOSED EMC FACILITY

Estimated Operating Expenses Monthly operating expenses for an EMC facility are predominantly fixed. The term *fixed expenses* means that sales activity has little or no effect on those expense categories. Salaries for both physicians and nonphysicians (e.g., receptionist, X-ray technician) must be paid regardless of patient visits. Rent, utility charges, and security services are similarly fixed expenses.

Monthly expenses for malpractice insurance are billed on a per patient basis (approximately $0.70/patient). Supply expenses also vary with the volume of patient visits and is, therefore, a variable expense. The supply cost per patient has historically averaged $4.67. The total variable cost per patient is then estimated at $5.37.

Deriving Sales Budgets The essence of the sales requirements approach is to develop a sales budget necessary to support the business. The breakeven sales budget is easily calculated from Exhibit 3-6. Estimated monthly fixed operating expenses are $26,350. The average patient charge at the original EMC is $37.00. Assuming the charge would average the same amount at the new facility, each patient visit will contribute $31.63 to these fixed expenses ($37.00 # $5.37 variable expenses). Therefore, a total of 833 patient visits per month will be required to break even ($26,350/$31.63). The breakeven point is graphically displayed in Exhibit 3-7.

The breakeven computation ignores financing costs. Regardless of the sources of capital used, a rate of return must be earned. If Dr. Petrillo personally supplies all the capital, he will require a rate of return. If in fact the required capital is borrowed from a commercial bank or an equipment leasing firm, the facility must generate revenues sufficient to cover interest expenses.

The required capital investment includes medical equipment ($51,000—Exhibit 3-3); office equipment ($13,500—Exhibit 2-4) and nonrecurring start-up expenses ($17,729—Exhibit 3-5). In addition to those capital requirements, oper-

Fixed Expenses

Advertising	2,000
Rent/utilities[1]	1,500
Legal/accounting	200
Manager salary	1,600
Nonphysician salaries	8,050[2]
Physician salaries	10,000
Postage	200
Security/housekeeping	250
Telephone	250
Depreciation[3]	1,075
Sundry	1,225
TOTAL FIXED EXPENSES	$26,350

Variable Expenses

Malpractice Insurance	$ .70 per patient
Supplies[4]	4.67 per patient
TOTAL VARIABLE EXPENSE PER PATIENT	$5.37

[1] $1,250/month rent + $250/month average utility expense
[2] Estimated at 115% of salaries to cover FUTA, FICA, Workmens' Compensation. amd state unemployment.
[3] Fixed assets of $64,000—straight line, 5-year life (60 months)
[4] Estimated from experience at EMC #1

**EXHIBIT 3-6   ESTIMATED MONTHLY OPERATING
EXPENSES FOR PROPOSED EMC FACILITY**

ating expenses in the early months will exceed revenue. If we establish, as a reserve, three months of operating expenses in the early months will exceed revenue. If we establish, as a reserve, three months of operating expenses, approximately $80,000 in additional captial will be required. Total start-up capital is, therefore, estimated at $162,229. At a cost of capital of 18 percent, the facility will have to generate an additional 129,300 per year or $2,450 per month to cover its captial costs.

Breakeven patient visits have been estimated at 833 patients per month. The sales budget to break even and cover anticipated capital costs would require 910 patients per month ($26,350 + $2350)/$31.63).

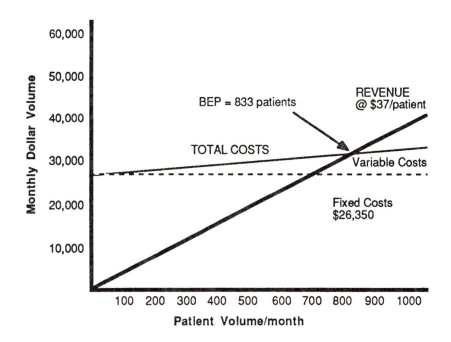

**EXHIBIT 3-7   BREAKEVEN ANALYSIS
FOR EMC FACILITY AT LOGAN**

Step 3. Judging Likely Market Share

A comparison of the results of Steps 1 and 2 indicates that of an estimated 43,000–48,000 annual patient visits in the trade area, EMC must capture a 23–25 percent market share to break even and cover its cost of capital. This share represents substantial market penetration.

The question facing Dr. Petrillo is, How likely is it that EMC could achieve such a market share? This is, of course, a complicated question. In order to formulate an answer, judgments regarding patient reactions and competitive reactions must be made.

EMC Competitive Advantages EMC offers convenient service without the usual appointment necessary for a doctor's office, or the usual wait at a hospital emergency department. Due to lower overhead expenses, EMC is less expensive than a hospital on virtually all procedures. The combined advantages of economy and convenience have contributed to a favorable reception in the original EMC trade area and in other cities around the country where EMC-type facilities have been opened.

Competition The trade area is served by a general hospital with an emergency department and eighteen physicians' offices. Several of the physicians practice specialties, such as obstetrics, and are not considered direct competitors of EMC. Nonetheless, 11 of the physicians either are general practitioners or practice family medicine. The EMC sales forecast will be affected by the behavior of these competitors. Faced with the entry of EMC into the market, how are these competitors likely to react?

In rapidly growing markets, the entry of a new competitor does not usually evoke a strong competitive response. The success of the new entrant is less a function of taking market share from existing competitors than it is of meeting a growing demand. Yet only under optimistic growth projections is it conceivable that EMC could prosper serving only new residents in the proposed site. EMC must attract patients from existing medical facilities. Physicians in private practice with established patient relationships are less likely to be injured by the entrance of EMC. However, because they generally view advertising and aggressive promotion activities as inappropriate, their likely response will be to "bad-mouth" EMC and raise questions regarding the quality of care offered. The hospital, as an institution with resources, and with the most to lose if EMC should enter, is expected to react more strongly. Hospitals have recently adopted advertising programs, modified fee schedules for minor emergencies, and changed staffing and triage activities to reduce waiting time in emergency departments. In short, the hospital, if forced, has the capabilities to negate EMC's competitive advantages.

In summary, EMC possesses some very real competitive advantages over traditional medical care providers. However, the hospital may react strongly to EMC's entrance into the market. Faced with high fixed costs of its own, the hospital administrators will be forced to do something if EMC approaches a 25 percent market share. Dr. Petrillo feels the operating plan of the facility must be changed in order to lower the breakeven market share. A review of the estimated operating expenses indicates that expenses can't be reduced. Based on the historical costs incurred at EMC #1, Dr. Petrillo feels these estimates are accurate, and to expect lower expenses is unrealistic. This focuses attention on the fee structure. By raising the fees on certain routine procedures and lab tests, the revenue per patient visit can be raised to $41 from $37. This will lower the breakeven market share to about 20 percent. This is considered an achievable level of penetration.

Step 4. Preparing the Forecasts

Due to the uncertainty surrounding the new facility, Dr. Petrillo and the EMC staff prepared three separate sales forecasts based on different assumptions of growth in the average number of patients treated per day. An optimistic forecast assumed that the breakeven member of patients per day would be reached in the sixth month of operations. A pessimistic forecast assumed it would take 14 months to reach breakeven patient flow and a conservative but likely forecast assumed month 10 to be the breakeven month.

Exhibit 3-8 is the sales forecast for the optimistic case. Once sales revenue is estimated it is a fairly straightforward task to project the estimated cash flows. Similar forecasts were

	Month 1	Month 2	Month 3	Month 4	Month 5	Month 6
Average patients/day	5	10	15	19	23	27
Revenue ($41/pt. visit)	6150	12300	18450	23370	28290	33210
Cash Received[1]	3998	9840	15683	20726	25399	30074
Cash Expenses[2]	26081	16886	27692	28335	28980	29625
Cash Gain (Loss)	(22083)	(17046)	(12009)	(7609)	(3581)	449
Cumulative Cash Position	(22083)	(39129)	(51138)	(58147)	(62328)	(61878)

	Month 7	Month 8	Month 9	Month 10	Month 11	Month 12
Average patients/day	30	33	35	37	38	39
Revenue ($41/pt. visit)	36900	40590	43050	45510	46740	47970
Cash Received	33948	37453	40159	42497	44034	45203
Cash Expenses	30108	30591	30913	31236	31397	31558
Cash Gain (Loss)	3840	6862	9245	11261	12637	13645
Cumulative Cash Position	(58038)	(51176)	(41931)	(30670)	(18033)	(4388)

[1] Estimated as: 65% Revenue received in 0-31 days
35% Revenue received in 31-60 days
5% Allowance for bad debts and adjustments

[2] Cash Expenses
= (Fixed Expenses - Depreciation + $5.37 (Patient Visits)
= 25275 + 5.37 per patient

EXHIBIT 3-8   EMERGENCY MEDICAL CENTER SALES AND CASH FLOW FORECAST OPTIMISTIC CASE: BREAKEVEN AT MONTH 6

prepared for the pessimistic and likely breakeven cases. By adding interest expenses into fixed costs, the same series of forecasts could be developed reflecting the cost of capital performance level as opposed to the breakeven performance level. Having gone through this forecasting effort, Dr. Petrillo commented:

The forecasting activity has provided us with a couple of advantages. First, it forced us to look hard at the market, the competition, and our cost structure. It also forced us to modify our fee schedule in light of those conditions. Second it gave us a rational basis for negotiating a line of credit with our bankers. They can see where the money is to go, how much we will need, and at what rate we will be able to pay the line down. Finally, the forecasts set some standards by which we can evaluate our progress. If we're behind our forecast come month 4 or 5, I know I'll have to get our credit line raised, and intensify our promotion efforts. It also gives my manager some targets to shoot for regarding expenses.

Chapter 4

Defining the
Target Market

The target market is composed of the principal customer groups to be served. The definition of these groups is essential to the evolution of market potential, which is discussed in Chapter 5. In addition, understanding who the target customer is has implications for a host of other decisions about the operation of a business. For instance, the type of customer to be served can affect the number and qualifications of the sales staff, the media through which you can communicate with the customer, and the location of the facility itself.

For these reasons, the definition of the target customers should be as precise as possible. It is likely that several customer groups will be served, each with distinct characteristics. In identifying customer groups it is useful to think in terms of the needs customers seek to satisfy and the purchasing power they must possess. Those individuals most likely to patronize the business can be thought of as the *primary target market*. These are the individuals that must be catered to in terms of pricing, hours of operation, and the other decisions identified in Figure 4-1.

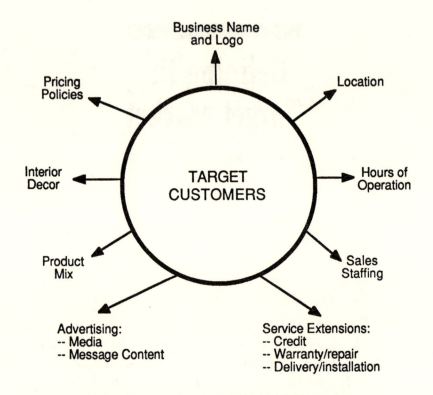

**FIGURE 4-1   DECISIONS INFLUENCED BY
THE TARGET MARKET DEFINITION**

The primary market for the EMC was identified as composed of families with several children, working women, and people without regular physicians. The extended hours, the no-appointment policy, and quick service of the EMC were designed to cater to these particular customer groups.

Secondary target markets will also generally exist. The individuals that make up secondary markets share some but not all of the characteristics of the primary targets. Their needs for the product or service may be less acute or their purchasing power may be questionable. While potential customers, it is less likely that they will be patrons.

A profile of the primary and secondary target customers is an attempt to identify measurable characteristics that indicate both the need and the ability to pay for the products or services being offered. In a retail business the target market is composed of individuals or households. In an industrial enterprise the target market is composed of other businesses. The concepts of primary and secondary target markets are relevant in either case, but the characteristics to be considered in developing a profile are quite different.

RETAIL MARKETS

The profile of a retail target market should consider

- *Demographic characteristics* such as age, sex, and marital status
- *Socioeconomic characteristics* such as occupation, family size, household income, and education
- *Housing characteristics* such as renter or owner, age of structure, and certain features including heating sources or construction materials
- *Psychological characteristics* such as security needs, peer group identification, status-seeking behavior, and style consciousness.
- *Purchase motivations* such as convenience or economy, and product characteristics such as durability or quality

The profile can also consider other products or services the "typical" customer might have purchased in the past. In other words, a target market may be identical to, or overlap with, an existing market. This is frequently the result of derived demand in which the target market demand is a function of other purchases. For example, boat owners, pet owners, recreational vehicle owners, hunting and fishing licensees, and VCR owners are in the target markets of marinas, veterinarians, and so on by virtue of their earlier purchase decisions.

In addition to derived demand, past purchases may indicate lifestyle, economic, or demographic characteristics that qualify for inclusion in the current target market. For example, dual-career and single-parent families who patronize day-care centers are also in the target market for house cleaning and lawn care services. Similarly, people who own individual retirement accounts (IRAs) are part of the target market for other investment services.

Of course, not every target market is definable on each of the categories of key characteristics. Some retail businesses serve customers with diverse demographic and/or socioeconomic characteristics. Nonetheless, our intent is to identify some distinguishing characteristics of the target customers.

INDUSTRIAL MARKETS

In the development of an industrial target market profile, the key characteristics are properties of businesses rather than properties of people. They include

- Organizational characteristics such as the industry in which the target customer firm participates, characteristics of the demand faced by the customer such as its seasonality, the size of the customer in terms of sales volume or the number of employees, and the customer's location
- Product characteristics such as the customer's end use, the size of the typical order, the frequency with which orders are placed, and permissible lead times
- Purchasing unit characteristics such as the decision process in selecting vendors, the pressures for economy that the purchasing unit may be under, and the degree of loyalty that may accrue to vendors.

The characteristics listed in Figure 4-3 are analogous to the individual demographics, socioeconomic, and other characteristics listed in Figure 4-2. Several of the characteristics are less intuitive and, therefore, merit additional discussion.

	Primary Target Markets	**Secondary Target Markets**
Demographics		
Age		
Sex		
Marital Status		
Socioeconomic		
Occupations		
Family Size		
Household Income		
Education Levels		
Housing		
Renter vs. Owner Occupied		
Residence Age		
Size (Sq. Ft., # Bedrooms)		
Location		
Psychological		
Fashion Conformity		
Upward Mobility		
Purchase Motivations		
Convenience		
Economy		
Quality-Oriented		
Reliability		
Other Likely Purchases:		

_____

_____

FIGURE 4-2   RETAIL TARGET CUSTOMER PROFILE WORKSHEET

Customer size, in terms of employment or sales volume, is a crucial variable in targeting industrial customers.

Large firms may not represent true opportunities. A variety of industrial products or services can be self-supplied if economical. As business firms grow, they tend to "internalize" the functions of some vendors. Self-supplied payroll services, security services, and some component parts can become economically feasible as the firm grows.

	Primary Target Markets	Secondary Target Markets

Organizational Characteristics
  Industry Type
  Seasonality of Demand
  Sales Volume
  Location
  Number of Employees

Product Characteristics
  End Use
  Order Size
  Frequency of Purchase
  Lead Times

Purchasing Unit Characteristics
  Decision Process
  Pressures for Economy
  Source Loyalty

**FIGURE 4-3   INDUSTRIAL TARGET
CUSTOMER PROFILE WORKSHEET**

Very small firms might not be profitable accounts. They may not generate enough purchase volume to justify selling expenses or the costs of servicing their accounts.

Because firms with industrial markets usually deal with fewer customers than those with retail markets, order size and order frequency are important characteristics of target customers.

The growing popularity of the just-in-time inventory system portends major changes in the operations of component parts suppliers, for example. A just-in-time system requires the delivery of small orders several times a shift directly to the assembly area. The customer, therefore, holds no inventory of components. Firms that select JIT manufacturers as customers have committed themselves to coordinated delivery schedules and the increased working capital required to hold their customers' components inventory. However, reduced selling costs, favorable payment schedules, coordinated production schedules, and a variety of other benefits can lead to an advantageous relationship for both organizations.

The point is not that small, frequent orders are good (bad), or that large, infrequent orders are bad (good); either customer group can be profitably served. The point is that order patterns received by industrial firms have such direct implications for every phase of operations that it is difficult to serve diverse customers efficiently.

Unlike retail firms, industrial organizations rarely deal with the ultimate consumer of their goods. They deal with intermediaries in a procurement or purchasing unit. Nonetheless, customer organizations have purchase motivations that are communicated through the purchasing representative. Quality, delivery, credit terms, reliability, and price all can come into play. Of course, which motivation will dominate the purchase decision depends on the nature of the product or service and the output market faced by the customer. For instance, price is likely to dominate when the cost of a component represents a substantial proportion of the customer's total cost and the customer sells in a competitive output market. Pressure on price will be less intense if costs can be passed on to the output market or if the component represents a small cost to the customer.

Industrial targets also differ from retail targets in that they generally enjoy less flexibility in changing vendors. As retail customers, we rarely incur any costs by changing our patronage to different retailers. Low change costs are not the rule among industrial customers. To change a supplier of a component part could result in machinery changes, product design changes, and retraining of employees. The costs of such operational changes can contribute to vendor loyalty, which is a desirable trait in a target customer.

Consider the examples of retail and industrial target market definitions presented in Figure 4-4. In particular, consider how the various operating decisions will be affected by the primary and secondary target definitions.

	Transient-Oriented Motel	Campus Typing/ Service	Furniture Importer/ Retailer	Medical Supplies Distribution	Computer Terminal Manufacturer	Specialty Steel Spring Manufacturer
Primary Targets	*Business auto traveler:* Self-employed Mfg. rep. Salesperson Economy minded "No frills"	*Graduate students' thesis* 300–500 pages 2 draft average Long lead time	*Young marrieds 25–35* Income > 30K Professionals college-educated Style and economy oriented	*Small hospitals* (under 200 beds) *Clinics, HMOs* (with over 75 patients visits per day)	*Graphics applications:* Design applications Major manufacturing and aerospace companies	U.S. Gov't Military aircraft applications Contract bids for new and replacement parts
Secondary Targets	*Vacation auto travelers:* Retired Young families, no children	*Student papers* 5–25 pages Short lead time *Faculty manuscripts during peak periods*	*Avant-garde/individualistic* Urban apt. dwellers Quality-oriented	*Physicians' offices:* Pediatrician General practice	*Interactive graphic market:* Companies with small to medium-size computers Drafting, data-analysis firms	Standardized parts demanded by OEM's in materials handling and construction equipment industries
Affected Operating Decisions	Location Pricing Room design Amenities	Promotion Fee structure Word processing equipment Pickup/delivery service	Product mix Location Credit terms Delivery/warranty Promotion	Product mix Sales force size Pricing Delivery service Credit terms	Product design After-sale support and training Installation Sales force Warranty Promotion	Production scheduling Vendor selection Sales and bid preparation Working capital financing Pricing Employment policies

FIGURE 4-4 ILLUSTRATIVE RETAIL AND INDUSTRIAL TARGET MARKET DEFINITIONS

Chapter 5

Estimating
Market Potential

In this chapter, the market potential side of our MP-SR forecasting method will be discussed in detail. Recall that our overall goal is to assess total market size objectively for the products or services being offered. Having defined the target market, two additional tasks must be performed in order to accomplish this goal.

1. The *trade area* that will be served must be delineated.
2. The *aggregate potential purchases* of the target customers within the trade area must be estimated.

TRADE AREA DEFINITION

The trade area represents the geographic territory from which the customers will be drawn. While the concept is relevant to all types of businesses, the trade areas of manufacturing and wholesaling businesses are determined by transportation and selling expenses. In retail businesses, the costs borne by customers in terms of travel time and expense define trade areas.

Trade areas can vary widely in size. A small grocery store may have as a trade area the immediate residential area surrounding it while an appliance store in the same block may draw customers from an entire community and perhaps even neighboring communities.

The factors that influence trade areas are numerous. The most important factors, however, can be narrowed down to four:

- Type of product or service
- Location of competition
- Traffic patterns and physical characteristics
- Compatibility with neighboring businesses

Type of Product or Service

Products and services fall into two general categories, each with its special implications for trade area definition.

Shopping Goods　*Shopping goods* are those products and services to which consumers will commit a significant amount of time before the purchase. Virtually all durable goods, such as automobiles and major appliances, are shopping goods. Clothing, stereo equipment, and investment services are other goods for which consumers are willing to spend time and effort in comparison shopping. In general, shopping goods are infrequently purchased products and services that consume a significant amount of a consumer's income.

Convenience Goods　*Convenience goods*, on the other hand, are those frequently purchased products and services that command little of our income, and therefore little of our time. Most food products, minor articles of clothing, pharmaceuticals, and personal care products are convenience goods.

This category includes impulse items such as those found at the checkout counter of the supermarket—to which we commit only a few seconds of thought before a purchase decision is made.

Because so little time is committed to convenience good purchases, the trade area for businesses selling such goods is small. Consumers will not travel or comparison shop and therefore will purchase at the closest location. Shopping goods, because they demand the consumer's attention, can draw from a larger trade area.

Degree of differentiation is an additional characteristic of products and services that influences trade area size. Differentiation means that a product enjoys some element of uniqueness. A product or service can be unique due to its design, quality, warranty, and so on. A business can be unique by virtue of the breadth of its product offerings, the knowledge of its sales personnel, or its customer services.

The notion of differentiation is implicit in the concept of shopping goods. Certainly if all car dealers and cars were identical—features, service, performance, price—it would make little sense to shop around. That is, in the absence of any differentiation, what may appear to be a shopping good can, in actuality, be a convenience good. For example, consider the decision to chose a bank for personal financial services. On the surface choosing a bank seems to be an important decision for a consumer. However, few of us commit much time to selecting a bank because the services they offer are not differentiated; they all offer the same things. It is, therefore, a convenience good and most of us go to the bank closest to our home or place of work.

Differentiated products or businesses will enjoy a larger trade area than those that are undifferentiated from competitors. That is why commercial banks need multiple branches, each of which serve an immediate trade area, and a 4-star restaurant can draw its clientele from an entire city.

Location of Competition

The proximity of competitors is a second factor that affects trade area definition. The effect, however, depends on the type of product or service being offered. In situations where undifferentiated products or services are being offered, the location of competitors can delineate the outer boundaries of a trade area. It is simply unreasonable to expect a customer to travel past one business in order to patronize another offering similar merchandise.

In the case of shopping goods, proximity can serve to increase the size of the trade area. The clustering of automobile dealerships in one section of town serves to attract customers from further away by facilitating the shopping behavior customers are expected to engage in. The recent emergence of retail personal computer stores is likely to follow the same pattern. By locating close to each other, the retailers have made it easier for consumers to shop and compare, thereby attracting customers from further distances.

Traffic Patterns and Physical Characteristics

Particularly important in retail trade areas are the predominant patterns in which people travel. This is, of course, greatly influenced by road and highway structures along with physical characteristics such as rivers and railway crossings. These characteristics influence travel time, a fundamental consideration in where people will choose to shop.

Compatibility with Neighboring Businesses

Compatibility is particularly important in mall locations but relevant to free-standing stores in shopping districts as well. The influence of compatibility in trade areas is similar to that of the auto dealers. By allowing consumers to conveniently and efficiently compare products and/or satisfy several shopping trips at once, the trade area is expanded.

Retail business in multistore locations is generated in three ways. First, traffic generated by the business itself. That is, customers who come to the mall or shopping district specifically to visit this particular retail location. The anchor tenants in malls, such as Sears, Penney's, Ward's, and other major department stores, are intended to be the principal generative businesses. Second is shared business, the business a retail store receives due to generating power of its neighbors. That is, business from people who are in the shopping area to visit another retailer. Finally, outlets can benefit from suscipient business, which is generated by people near a store for purposes other than shopping. Luncheonettes in downtown office districts, gift shops in hotels and hospitals, and concessions in train and airport terminals exist primarily on suscipient business.

Methods of Trade Area Definition

Distance and Drive Time Plots   Based on the factors discussed above, the maximum distance a consumer might travel can be estimated. In urban areas, drive time may be more meaningful than distance. In either case, distance or drive time can be plotted on a map to define the trade area.

License Plate Analysis   A useful technique for delineating a trade area of mall locations is to analyze a sample of the automobile license plates in the parking lot. Addresses acquired through motor vehicle registrations can then be plotted on a map.

Newspaper Circulation Data   Because newspapers are an important advertising medium, circulation density is a reasonably accurate reflection of the overall trade area. This approach is particularly useful in deciding whether or not the residents of a neighboring community should be included in a trade area definition. If 6 out of every 10 households within the city receive the daily newspaper but only 1 out of 10 households in a neighboring community receive the city's newspaper, those residents are not being attracted to the city to shop and are outside the trade area.

Customer Spotting   Intercepting shoppers in a mall or shopping district to establish the neighborhood or section of town in which they reside can also serve to define a trade area. The responses would be plotted in the same fashion as the license plate analysis.

Interviews with anchor store managers, mall managers, and operators of neighboring businesses   Individuals who are already operating within the trade area may have very clear ideas about the boundaries. Store managers at anchor locations can analyze credit card purchases, or may have conducted consumer surveys among their customers. Mall managers frequently sponsor shopper surveys for the purpose of identifying the mall's trade area.

Case Study 5-1—The Locker Room

The Locker Room is a successful retail sporting goods operation. They have been in business for over four years, and continue to grow. An opportunity for a second location in a nearby town has come up.

A real estate broker has informed the owner, Rick Jones, of a vacancy in a relatively new shopping center. The center has a major mass merchandiser as an anchor tenant. It also has a floorcovering retailer, a hair salon, and a popular fast-food franchise. The trade area is, however, not known. Rick has interviewed the managers of the neighboring businesses, but there is not much agreement about where the shopping center patrons are drawn from. The center is close to a major city and

Interviewer: _____ Date: _____ Time: _____

Instructions: Approach each shopping party as they leave the center and approach their vehibles. Inquire *politely* as to what city or town they live in.

	Residence	# of People in party
1.		
2.		
3.		
4.		
5.		
6.		
7.		
8.		
9.		
10.		
11.		
12.		
13.		
14.		
15.		
16.		
17.		
18.		
19.		
20.		
21.		
22.		
23.		
24.		
25.		
26.		
27.		
28.		
29.		
30.		

EXHIBIT 5-1   INTERVIEWING SHEET FOR CUSTOMER SPOTTING STUDY

is surrounded by several towns with shopping facilities. Before Rick can make a decision on the new location, he must determine the trade area.

Rick designed a customer-spotting study in which customers will be intercepted in the shopping center and asked where they live.

Rick has hired two college students to do the interviewing. He decides to intercept customers over a two week period. The interviewing schedule should include weekend and weekdays, day and evening hours. He sends his interviewers, equipped with clipboards, out on Tuesday evening, Saturday afternoon, Thursday morning, and the following Friday evening. Rick has instructed them to intercept the first 75 shopping parties they see during each interviewing session. The form of the questionnaire is given as Exhibit 5-1.

After tabulating the 300 interviews, Rick can define the trade area (Exhibit 5-2). Most customers live within a 2.5-mile radius of the center. The results indicate that the center clearly does not draw much from the major city or its largest suburb. Rick now realizes he will have to rely on the immediate small-town populations for sales at the new location.

DETERMINING MARKET POTENTIAL

Once the target market is profiled and the trade area is defined, estimates of total market potential can be made. A variety of information sources are available to help pinpoint consumption behavior. In general, we must search for estimates of purchase size and purchase frequency. Measures of these attributes can be in the form of

- Average expenditures per person or per household in the product/service category
- Average number of purchases per month or year
- Total dollar expenditures in the product/service category
- Number of people or households within the trade area that fit the target demographic profile

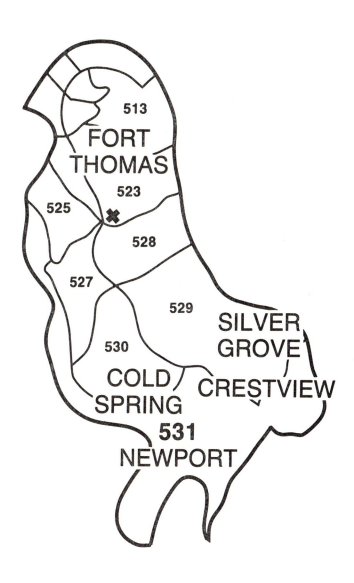

EXHIBIT 5-2   THE LOCKER ROOM TRADE AREA

The search for this type of information requires some investigation skills. Contact with trade associations, equipment suppliers, and wholesalers and distributors, and the resourceful use of published statistics from government and commercial sources can all contribute to the identification of aggregate market potential.

Trade Associations

Most industries have organized associations to represent the interests of industry members. Many associations serve multiple functions, including lobbying various local, state, and federal bodies to present the positions of industry members in legislative proceedings. Associations also collect and disseminate information on market trends and economic conditions that affect the industry. Further, trade associations have as part of their mission the promotion of the industry. Because they are in contact with industry members, they can provide a wealth of information useful to someone considering entering the industry. Ideas for promotions or advertising, trade area sizes, purchase frequency, customer profiles, pricing strategies, and lists of potential suppliers are often available. Of course, the availability of such information varies from association to association. In general, the larger the industry, the more sophisticated the research function of the trade association will be. Directories of trade associations are presented in Appendix A.

Equipment Suppliers

In industries that require investment in special equipment, and in particular when the equipment represents a substantial capital investment, equipment suppliers can be valuable sources of information. They have an interest in selling you equipment, and their well-being is a function of your business and the other businesses they supply. Because of their position in the industry, equipment suppliers have seen both failures and successes. They frequently have formulated some site considerations, rules for trade area definition, and profiles of your target customer.

Wholesalers and Distributors

Similar to equipment suppliers, wholesalers and product distributors view you as a potential customer. They supply a number of other businesses, perhaps even some competitors. They are usually quite knowledgeable about seasonal trends, pricing, and inventory levels. Some wholesalers can also direct you to used equipment, such as display racks, that may be available due to the failure or remodeling of the facility of another customer. They can also be a source of capital for inventory financing. Again, the basis for their cooperation and assistance is that their well-being and growth is dependent on people like you.

Newspapers and Broadcast Media

Local newspapers, TV, and radio media have a vested interest in maintaining a thorough understanding of local retail markets. In order to attract national and local advertising dollars, the media must be able to describe their market accurately. They generally analyze a wealth of demographic data concerning the local population. They also sponsor surveys of their readers/listeners/viewers to identify shopping behavior and consumer expenditures for various goods and services. As a potential advertiser, data generated by their research departments will generally be made available.

Government Documents

Local, state, and federal governments monitor business conditions and demographic trends for purposes of planning and estimating their revenues. All of these data are compiled at taxpayer expense and are, therefore, public information.

At the federal level, the *Census of Population, Census of Housing,* and *Census of Business* are particularly useful for estimating market potential. The unit of analysis in these data is generally the county level. Unfortunately, county boundaries don't always conform to trade area definitions. Frequently some judgments on segmenting or aggregating county data must be made. Despite this drawback, published government data are considered some of the most reliable data available.

In larger metropolitan areas some federal data are available on a *census tract* basis. Tracts are relatively small subdivisions of city that have visible borders, such as streets, and are homogeneous with respect to economic conditions. Tracts usually have between 2500 and 8000 residents. Because of their small size, a trade area can usually be approximated by adding several together. (See Case Study 5-2 at the end of this chapter.)

✓Data from government documents that are useful for our purposes include

- Population and household counts
- Age distributions of residents
- Occupational distributions
- Family and per capita income
- Educational levels
- Payroll statistics
- Housing characteristics
- Aggregate expenditures in various retail trade categories

Commercial Data Sources

A number of companies are engaged in the collection and dissemination of market data for profit. Some data are quite expensive compared to government sources, but they are frequently in a more useful form than government data. One readily available, and inexpensive, source is the annual *Survey of Buying Power*, a sample of which is presented in Figure 5-1. Other commercial data sources are listed in Appendix A.

While most published data sources are available in public libraries and college and university libraries, several types of organizations serve as "clearing houses" for market data. Before plunging into the various forms of census data yourself or purchasing commercially published data, it is well worth your time to investigate the local Chamber of Commerce and your state's Small Business Development Center. Your local Chamber exists to promote commerce in your market area. Similar to the trade associations, part of their mission is to assist new and existing businesses. A Chamber in a larger business community is likely to maintain a library of information and provide compilations of relevant information from a variety of published sources.

Small Business Development Centers (SBDC's) are statewide programs jointly sponsored by the host state and the federal Small Business Administration. They provide data and consulting services in an effort to promote the development of small business. Not all states have an SBDC, but your local Chamber or state economic development office can advise you about the availability of such services in your area.

1983 RETAIL SALES BY STORE GROUP—WITH 1977 CENSUS DATA

ESTIMATES: 1983   U.S. CENSUS: 1977

METRO AREA / County	Year	Total Retail Sales ($000)	Food Stores Total ($000)	Food Stores Super-markets ($000)	Eating & Drinking Places Total ($000)	General Merchandise Total ($000)	General Merchandise Department Stores ($000)	Apparel & Accessories Stores Total ($000)	Furniture/Home Furnishings/Appliance Stores Total ($000)	Furniture & Home Furn. ($000)	Automotive Dealers Total ($000)	Gasoline Service Stations Total ($000)	Bldg. Mtls. & Hardware Dealers Total ($000)	Drug-stores Total ($000)
NEW HAMPSHIRE														
MANCHESTER - NASHUA	1983	1,812,289	412,439	389,520	186,667	220,664	182,802	95,305	93,067	56,812	287,480	156,663	110,747	50,697
	1977	1,014,337	228,425	215,153	75,141	129,191	107,679	49,355	41,958	26,611	206,393	68,180	60,331	24,459
Hillsborough	1983	1,812,289	412,439	389,520	186,667	220,664	182,802	95,305	93,067	56,812	287,480	156,663	110,747	50,697
	1977	1,014,337	228,425	215,153	75,141	129,191	107,679	49,355	41,958	26,611	206,393	68,180	60,331	24,459
PORTSMOUTH - DOVER - ROCHESTER	1983	1,954,974	508,918	479,768	202,283	185,959	144,399	89,115	90,777	47,617	298,099	142,304	107,632	59,184
	1977	1,032,578	260,985	245,376	31,080	100,865	77,883	42,080	37,043	19,884	194,755	63,240	67,878	24,743
Rockingham	1983	1,465,324	391,952	369,510	153,996	146,418	123,742	73,158	71,403	40,407	214,439	99,187	79,976	37,929
	1977	764,620	197,738	185,916	60,349	75,738	63,978	32,893	27,137	16,082	141,748	46,313	50,992	15,682
Strafford	1983	489,650	116,966	110,258	48,287	39,541	20,657	15,957	19,374	7,210	83,660	43,117	27,656	21,255
	1977	267,958	63,247	59,460	20,731	25,127	13,905	9,187	9,906	3,812	53,007	16,927	16,886	9,061
ALL COUNTIES														
Belknap	1983	323,330	86,086	82,412	31,919	25,648	18,287	13,430	16,748	6,922	47,090	23,884	38,065	6,768
	1977	183,572	44,478	42,339	12,913	12,808	9,175	7,866	6,845	2,937	38,556	11,085	22,914	3,561
Carroll	1983	201,958	51,370	47,723	27,039	10,203	4,322	6,115	7,746	4,782	16,416	16,811	26,291	3,627
	1977	116,662	29,906	27,060	12,592	5,521	2,452	3,761	3,749	2,393	14,220	9,342	14,111	1,885
Cheshire	1983	301,676	79,459	76,877	30,249	26,377	15,188	9,974	13,120	6,702	44,702	26,817	17,323	5,277
	1977	188,351	51,611	49,652	14,312	17,586	10,627	5,389	6,659	3,532	33,703	13,055	13,055	3,071
Coos	1983	187,234	50,505	48,079	18,173	17,527	12,376	5,554	5,881	3,595	25,221	18,750	13,346	4,629
	1977	117,137	30,700	29,061	7,863	10,535	7,606	3,589	3,086	1,960	22,039	8,765	8,886	2,461
Grafton	1983	481,134	135,047	131,162	42,524	50,721	38,438	18,132	20,194	12,085	48,812	49,217	27,193	8,622
	1977	263,124	69,813	67,420	19,115	28,917	22,145	9,070	9,369	5,829	36,483	22,047	16,155	5,251
Hillsborough	1983	1,812,289	412,439	389,520	186,667	220,664	182,802	95,305	93,067	56,812	287,480	156,663	110,747	50,697
	1977	1,014,337	228,425	215,153	75,141	129,191	107,679	49,355	41,958	26,611	206,393	68,180	60,331	24,459
Merrimack	1983	675,997	165,020	155,942	51,378	84,199	49,526	16,847	20,583	12,126	108,073	91,347	42,707	18,429
	1977	356,071	76,058	20,702	23,818	41,636	25,527	9,128	9,307	5,729	77,055	34,532	25,682	8,855
Rockingham	1983	1,465,324	391,952	369,510	153,996	146,418	123,742	73,158	71,403	40,407	214,439	99,187	79,976	37,929
	1977	764,620	197,738	185,916	60,349	75,738	63,978	32,893	27,137	16,082	141,748	46,313	50,992	15,682
Strafford	1983	489,650	116,966	110,258	48,287	39,541	20,657	15,957	19,374	7,210	83,660	43,117	27,656	21,255
	1977	267,958	63,247	59,460	20,731	25,127	13,905	9,187	9,906	3,812	53,007	16,927	16,886	9,061
Sullivan	1983	172,406	44,891	44,524	12,853	8,974	5,760	10,110	7,976	2,882	28,530	12,406	19,233	6,512
	1977	115,640	29,723	29,425	5,784	6,129	4,061	5,175	4,251	1,619	25,354	7,005	13,939	3,582
TOTAL METRO COUNTIES	1983	3,767,263	921,357	869,288	388,950	406,623	327,201	184,420	183,844	104,429	585,579	298,967	218,379	109,881
	1977	2,047,915	489,410	460,520	156,221	230,056	185,562	91,435	79,001	46,505	401,148	131,420	128,209	49,202
TOTAL STATE	1983	6,110,998	1,533,735	1,456,007	603,085	630,272	471,098	264,582	276,092	153,523	904,423	538,199	402,537	163,745
	1977	3,387,452	825,643	781,544	252,618	353,188	267,155	135,413	122,267	70,504	648,558	237,251	240,241	77,868

FIGURE 5-1 SURVEY OF BUYING POWER

Case Study 5-2—The Floral Supply

Charles and Regina Clay operate a wholesale floral supply business serving a number of retail floral shops in a 75-mile-wide area. The demand for their line of products is a function of the market potential in the trade areas served by each of their customers and the number of customers they supply. In order to formulate a sales forecast for the wholesale business, they began estimating the retail market potential of each of their customers.

Recently, a well-established retail shop in their market area's largest city had changed ownership. The new owners were energetic and aggressive, and committed to expanding the retail volume of the business. The new owners were interested in having the Clays as a vendor and had provided Charles and Regina with what appeared to be very optimistic sales projections. To determine the value of the new account, Regina formulated an estimate of the market potential in retail trade area of their new customer.

Regina contacted Florists Transworld Delivery Association (FTD) and secured a wealth of information regarding the retail flower business. She knew from her previous experience and her own shopping behavior that about a 10-minute drive time was the limit that people would travel for floral products. She plotted that drive time out on a map. The defined area corresponded pretty closely to the fifteen census tracts outlined in Exhibit 5-3.

At the nearby university library she referenced the *Census of Population and Housing* and added across the fifteen tracts to develop a profile of the trade-area residents, as shown in Exhibit 5-4.

The FTD *Flower Business Fact Book* that Regina received contained information on per capita floral expenditures by state and region of the country (Exhibit 5-5). A quick estimate of mar-

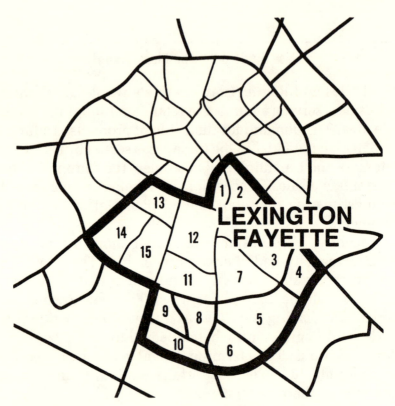

EXHIBIT 5-3   THE FLORAL SUPPLY TRADE AREA

Population and Age
Total persons	65,307	
18 years and older	49,555	(76%)
25–44 years	17,960	(27.5%)

Education of Adults over 25 years
Total Adults	38,894	
High School Grads	9,572	
Some College	8,470	
College Grads	15,037	(39%)

Household Income
Total Households	25,876	
Income $25,000 or more	8,920	(39%)

**EXHIBIT 5-4   THE FLORAL SUPPLY TRADE AREA
DEMOGRAPHIC CHARACTERISTICS**

ket potential within the trade area indicates that the annual potential is 65,307 people times $15.94 per person = $1,040,993.

Other information provided by FTD is based on shopper surveys that gauge the frequency of purchase and focus on target market definitions. It is estimated that shoppers fall into 3 categories: light, medium and heavy purchasers. Light purchasers buy flowers 1 to 2 times per year and represent 25 percent of flower customers. Medium purchasers buy 3 to 5 times per year and represent 36 percent of customers. Finally, heavy purchasers buy flowers 6 to 7 times a year and represent 37 percent of flower customers.

With this information Regina set out to estimate the trade area market potential from a different perspective in order to get a sense of the accuracy of the 1 million dollar figure.

All adults are potential flower customers; but the primary age group, according to FTD, is 25–49 years of age. Of people in this age group, almost 60 percent are flower purchasers. Regina knows there are 17,960 people in the 25–44 year age bracket within the trade area, and she made the following computation:

```
17,960 people × .60 = 10,776 flower customers
    10,766 × .25 = 2,695 light purchasers
    10,766 × .36 = 3,879 medium purchasers
    10,766 × .37 = 3,987 heavy purchasers
```

The proportion of other adults that are purchasers is less than 60 percent—but Regina isn't sure how much less. She is willing to assume that 40 percent of the younger and older adult age groups are flower customers. By subtracting the 25–44 population from the population over 18, she estimates there are 31,595 people in the other age groups within the trade area.

```
31,595 people × .40 = 12,638 flower customers
    12,638 × .25 = 3,159 light purchasers
    12,638 × .36 = 4,550 medium purchasers
    12,638 × .37 = 4,676 heavy purchasers
```

**PER CAPITA EXPENDITURES
BY REGIONS/STATE FOR THE UNITED STATES
1980**

REGION/STATES	AVERAGE PER CAPITA EXPENDITURE FOR 1980	REGION/STATES	AVERAGE PER CAPITA EXPENDITURE FOR 1980
New England Region	$14.10	West South Central Region	$15.73
Connecticut	14.86	Arkansas	14.82
Maine	11.93	Louisiana	13.39
Massachusetts	14.53	Oklahoma	15.90
New Hampshire	13.41	Texas	16.54
Rhode Island	14.49	South Atlantic Region	$15.47
Vermont	10.04	Delaware	15.87
Mid Atlantic Region	$13.24	District of Columbia	24.73
New Jersey	13.99	Florida	15.53
New York	11.83	Georgia	16.15
Pennsylvania	14.86	Maryland	14.99
East North Central Region	$15.29	North Carolina	15.46
Illinois	17.38	South Carolina	12.36
Indiana	15.44	Virginia	14.60
Michigan	14.67	West Virginia	18.65
Ohio	14.82	Mountain Region	$14.62
Wisconsin	12.31	Arizona	12.46
West North Central Region	$14.99	Colorado	16.19
Iowa	15.94	Idaho	15.50
Kansas	17.12	Montana	13.43
Minnesota	13.87	Nevada	19.54
Missouri	14.97	New Mexico	10.91
Nebraska	14.49	Utah	15.56
North Dakota	14.98	Wyoming	16.16
South Dakota	11.60	Pacific Region	$14.37
East South Central Region	$15.38	Alaska	17.00
Alabama	14.76	California	13.70
Kentucky	15.94	Hawaii	24.71
Mississippi	13.16	Oregon	14.16
Tennessee	16.66	Washington	15.62
		TOTAL U.S. AVERAGE	$14.79

Source: *Flower Business Fact Book* (1982 edition)

EXHIBIT 5-5   FTD FLOWER FACTS BOOK

The average flower purchase has historically been $10 but it is probably higher today. Nonetheless, Regina chooses to be conservative and use the $10 figure. By estimating the number of people in each purchaser category she can now estimate total trade area volume.

Number of people	×	Average # of purchases per year	×	$10 per purchase	=	Dollar Volume
5853 light	×	1.5	×	$10	=	$ 87,795
8429 medium	×	4.0	×	$10	=	$337,160
8663 heavy	×	6.5	×	$10	=	$556,095
			Estimated Total Volume		=	$981,050

It appears from two different estimates that the total market potential of their new customer is about one million dollars. That potential sales volume translates into an attractive wholesale account.

Case Study 5-3—WXXX-FM

Tom Payne recently joined the staff of WXXX as sales manager. WXXX is an FM radio station located in a medium-sized market. The station emphasizes an adult contemporary program format, which is the most popular format among top stations in the fifty largest retail markets.

Station management subscribes to the ARBITRON rating service, which measures listenership in various metropolitan markets. The most recent survey indicates that WXXX-FM is seventh in average listenership in the market. Most distressing to the station's owners is the fact that two other stations with adult contemporary formats are ranked numbers three and six in average listenership. The other stations that rank above WXXX program country, easy listening, and album-oriented rock formats and, therefore, are targeting slightly different audiences.

The programming director is determined to improve listenership. A variety of plans have been formulated, including the introduction of several new syndicated features and expanded reviews of local theater, film, and concert events.

As the new sales manager, Tom has been charged with analyzing the current sales strategy and making recommendations for its improvement. Tom has contacted the National Association of Broadcasters in Washington, D.C., and received information on the operating characteristics of FM stations similar in size around the country. Stations equivalent to WXXX received about 73 percent of their sales revenue from the advertising time sold to local retail and service firms. An additional 22 percent of revenue comes from national advertisers buying specific = "spots" to promote their products. The balance of the revenue is the result of network radio sales.

In analyzing WXXX revenue flows, Tom has determined that their share of local advertising dollars is not up to par. Because advertising expenditures are a function of retail trade activity, Tom decides to analyze the Dayton market in order to estimate retail potential.

The trade area of WXXX encompasses its metro area, and is made up of two counties. The area comforms to the Standard Metropolitian Statistical Area (SMSA) that is defined by the federal government. Based on the Census of Retail Trade and Census of Service Industries, Tom has estimated that their metro area represents a retail and service market of almost $5 billion (Exhibit 5-6).

Based on the estimated retail and service volume, Tom can estimate what total advertising expenditures to support such volume might be. He and his radio broadcasting colleagues also have some rules of thumb with which they can estimate radio's share of total advertising expenditures.

Tom also prepared a demographic profile of the metro area for his salespeople to use as a selling tool with retailers (Exhibit 5-7).

Retail *(5861 establishments)*	**Sales (000's)**
Building materials, hardware, garden supply	130,292
General merchandise	479,334
Food stores	843,991
Automotive dealers	637,087
Gasoline service stations	414,392
Apparel and accessory stores	155,651
Furniture, home furnishings	162,530
Eating and drinking places	383,571
Drug and proprietary stores	104,188
Miscellaneous retail (liquor, sporting goods, pets, etc.)	327,060
Total Retail	3,638,096

Services *(4100 establishments)*	
Hotel, motel	55,344
Personal services (laundry, beauty)	98,639
Business service (photocopy, computer services)	373,335
Auto repair, services	96,739
Miscellaneous repair (electronics, jewelry)	62,312
Amusement and recreation services	53,227
Health services (except hospitals)	368,914
Legal services	73,856
Engineering, architectural services	57,593
Accounting, bookkeeping services	42,845
Social and other services (daycare)	13,358
Selected educational services	5,073
Total services	1,301,235
Total retail and services	4,939,331

Sources: 1982 Census of Retail Trade—Geographic Area Series
1982 Census of Service Industries—Geographic Area Series

**EXHIBIT 5-6   SUMMARY OF RETAIL AND
SERVICE ACTIVITY IN WXXX'S SMSA**

Population   830,070

Households   300,133   (66% owner occupied;
                                             33% renter)

Income per household $20,583

Income per capita $ 7,511

Retail expenditures $3.6 mill.

Retail sales per household $12,122

Adult Contemporary Age
Group Target 33–48 years old   9328   (12% of total pop.)

Education (persons over 25):
    High school graduate = 69.9%
    Some college or college graduate = 30.3%

Commuting characteristics (workers over 16):
    Drive alone to work = 74.3%
    Average drive travel time = 19.3 minutes

Sources: 1980 Census of Population

EXHIBIT 5-7   DEMOGRAPHIC PROFILE OF WXXX-FM'S SMSA

Chapter 6

Deriving Sales Requirements

In Chapter 5 the market potential, or "top-down" component of our forecasting system, was developed. This chapter will focus on the other side of the MP-SR method.

The objective of the sales requirements procedure is to estimate the level of sales activity necessary to support the business venture. The sales estimate is usually formulated at several performance levels.

The *breakeven* sales budget represents the minimal performance standard. Estimated sales revenue in the breakeven case would be sufficient to meet the operating expenses of the business, but would provide no operating profit.

The *cost-of-capital* sales budget incorporates not only operating expenses but also a profit margin representing a return on invested funds. The desired rate of return can vary, even in similar ventures, reflecting different expectations on the part of the owners/investors. As a practical matter, the minimum rate of return should equal the prevailing interest rate charged by commercial banks for unsecured loans. The cost-of-capital budget estimates a sales volume that ensures the long-term survival of the firm.

If a firm enjoys a sales volume that allows it to meet its operating expenses and pay its creditors and investors an adequate return on the funds contributed to the venture, it is operating at what economists term the "normal" profit level. Under most circumstances, a firm is economically viable if operating at this level.

In order to derive the sales budgets, start-up and operating expenses must be estimated. As with any planning effort, the development of these expense schedules requires that some assumptions and estimates be made. The data sources listed can be investigated to ensure that most equipment costs and other expense estimates are reasonably accurate. When in doubt, however, be conservative and on the high side.

ESTIMATING START-UP EXPENSES

One-time expenses incurred at the onset of a venture fall into two principal categories:

- Fixed asset requirements
- Nonrecurring start-up expenses

Fixed Asset Requirements

Capital required for the purchase of necessary equipment, fixtures, and other depreciable assets is not difficult to estimate. Most individuals contemplating a new venture or the expansion of an existing business have a pretty clear understanding of equipment needs. The other major categories of fixed assets include office furniture and fixtures, signs, and the cost of leasehold improvements. A worksheet is provided as Figure 6-1.

Leasehold Improvements   _____

Equipment Total   _____

   (Itemize)   _____

                               _____

                               _____

                               _____

Office Equipment Total   _____

   Desks   _____

   Filing Cabinets   _____

   (Etc.)   _____

Fixtures (shelving, display racks, etc.)   _____

Exterior Signs   _____

Total Fixed Asset Requirements $ _____

FIGURE 6-1   FIXED ASSET REQUIREMENTS WORKSHEET

Nonrecurring Start-up Expenses

These expenses represent costs associated with getting a venture off the ground. They occur only once, and with the exception of the beginning inventory and office supplies, do not represent physical assets. All of these expenses will be incurred before the business collects any sales revenue and therefore must be financed out of start-up capital. Notice that to complete the worksheet in Figure 6-2, considerable thought must be given to inventories, staffing, and initial promotion effort.

Legal and Accounting Fees _____

Consulting Fees _____

Product Development and/or Testing _____

Utility Deposits _____

Lease Deposits _____

Staff Training _____

Insurance Prepayments _____

Office Supplies _____

Beginning Inventory _____

Initial Promotion Budget _____

Total Nonrecurring Start-up Expenses $ _____

FIGURE 6-2 NONRECURRING START-UP EXPENSES WORKSHEET

ESTIIMATING OPERATING EXPENSES

The final schedule of expenses that must be estimated is the recurring costs associated with the operation of the business. These include rent and utilities, payroll, supplies, advertising, and so on.

Many of the operating expenses in Figure 6-3 are self-explanatory. However, four of them require special consideration when estimates are being formed: payroll taxes and fringes, advertising, interest, and depreciation.

Payroll Taxes and Fringes

As an employer, you are obligated to make contributions to F.I.C.A. (Social Security), F.U.T.A. (federal unemployment),

Rent   _____

Utilities   _____

Telephone   _____

Insurance   _____

Manager Salary   _____

Staff Salaries   _____

Payroll Taxes and Fringes   _____

Advertising   _____

Supplies   _____

Interest Charges   _____

Depreciation   _____

Total Monthly Operating Expenses $ _____

FIGURE 6-3   MONTHLY OPERATING EXPENSES WORKSHEET

and your state unemployment insurance, and you must purchase Workers' Compensation insurance. All are computed as rates on gross pay, and with the exception of F.I.C.A. can vary by type of business, the experience of your firm, and the state in which you operate. For planning purposes, 15 percent of gross payroll will be sufficient to cover these expenses in most beginning firms.

In addition to these mandated expenses, benefits offered (such as paid vacations and holidays, sick leave, and group insurance coverage) will also add to total labor expenses. If any of these benefits are planned as part of the compensation system, an additional 5 percent of gross payroll should be expensed (20 percent total).

✓*Advertising*

Establishing an advertising budget is one of the more complex and consuming tasks in business planning. The advertising program goes right to the heart of what the business is attempting to be for the target customer. Because advertising can be a significant expense and because the success of the business will depend on how much and how effectively money is spent, this budget demands management attention.

Unfortunately, there is no handy rule of thumb or easy answer to the question of how large an ad budget should be. Differences in businesses, markets, competitive situations, and media costs make it impossible to formulate a decision rule. There are, however, four basic approaches to setting a budgeted advertising expenditure, none of which is entirely satisfactory.

Objective Task   The objective-task approach is the most rational in that the budget is directly related to specific communication objectives. The approach requires that objectives for the ad program be established. The media and frequency necessary to achieve the objectives are then determined along with the respective costs. The objectives can involve a variety of concerns, such as improving customer awareness, increasing sales levels, or building store traffic. Translating the objectives into a media schedule is the major difficulty with this approach. The assistance of advertising professionals, either ad agency or media representatives, is usually necessary. For instance, to build store traffic for an "end of season" clearance sale might translate into a package of 25 ten-second radio spots during morning and afternoon drive times and a series of display advertisements in the local newspaper.

The appeal of this approach is that the communication needs of the firm are identified first and costs considered second. Rather than the ad effort being tailored to existing funds, it is tailored to the needs of the business. In practice, this approach often leads to forecasted expenditures that are beyond the means of the firm. However, by modifying the objectives an affordable budget can be developed.

Percent of Sales   The percent of sales approach is perhaps the most commonly used method for budgeting. Here total advertising expenditures are set at a fixed percentage of historical or forecasted sales. Most retail and service firms spend between 1 percent and 5 percent of sales on advertising. In this approach an arbitrary proportion is determined, say 3 percent, and applied to the previous year's sales revenue or to some forecasted level to establish a budget. Simplicity is the major advantage of this approach, although it also provides control so that expenditures don't get out of hand. The drawback to the percent-of-sales approach is that the budget is established with no regard for the particular communication needs of your firm in your market.

Meet the Competition   Setting a budget to meet the competition presumes that if you're competing for the same customers, you have the same communication requirements. In some situations this may well be true. However, imitating competitors who may advertise ineffectively or who enjoy long-established reputations in the marketplace doesn't make much sense. The drawback, here again, is that the budget is based on the competitors' communication needs rather than your own. Nonetheless, to view a respected competitor's efforts as a budgetary guide can be a useful practice.

All We Can Afford   The "all we can afford" approach is the weakest of the four approaches. This treats advertising as an expense rather than a marketing tool. As with the percent of sales approach, advertising would be cut during periods of low sales and raised during peak periods. This could be just the opposite of what is desirable.

The objective-task approach, tempered by knowledge of what your competitors are doing or what similar firms in your line of business are doing, is the best approach for our purposes.

Interest Expenses

In order to estimate interest expenses, knowledge of the total capital requirements and financing arrangements are necessary.

Total capital requirements can be estimated as the sum of total fixed assets requirements *plus* the total nonrecurring start-up expenses *plus* some reserve to cover operating expenses. The reserve is necessary because in the early months of the venture sales volume is not likely to be sufficient to meet rent, payroll, and other monthly obligations. For planning purposes, a three month reserve should be considered as adequate. However, in some ventures a larger reserve might be appropriate.

The total capital requirements *minus* the amount of capital to be contributed by owners equals the estimated amount to be financed by outside sources. Monthly interest expenses can be computed on that amount.

Depreciation

Depreciation represents the cost of "consuming" the fixed assets used in the operation of the business. As with other expenses (such as materials, labor, or supplies) that are charged against the revenue they helped generate, some portion of the fixed assets must also be recognized periodically as an expense. Unlike other expenses, depreciation is a noncash expense. It doesn't represent a monthly cash outflow from the business, since the display racks, equipment, and other fixed assets were, obviously, paid for during start-up. Nonetheless, the cost of the assets must be recognized if the true profit picture of the business is to be estimated.

If the full cost of fixed assets were expensed against the first month's revenue, the profit picture would be understated. Similarly, if we ignore the cost of fixed assets, we would overstate the profits of the firm. The determination of a depreciation schedule that establishes the value of fixed assets to be expensed each month is governed by tax considerations. For planning purposes, straight-line depreciation, in which a constant proportion of cost is charged each month of the estimated useful life of the asset, is appropriate.

DATA SOURCES

In constructing the expense schedules a variety of data sources can be drawn upon:

- New and used equipment dealers, and their sales brochures and catalogs
- Contractors
- Equipment leasing firms
- Office supply firms
- Utilities
- Advertising agencies
- Chambers of Commerce
- Suppliers and wholesalers
- Bankers
- Insurance agents
- Trade associations
- Published financial studies

Most of these data sources are either self-explanatory or were discussed in detail in the previous chapter. However, published financial statement studies can be so valuable that they merit some additional consideration.

Statement studies are based on the aggregation of profit-and-loss statements and balance-sheet information drawn from similar businesses. For example, the operating characteristics of small retail florists are presented in Figure 6-4.

These data were collected from a group of retail florists and compiled to provide some benchmark information. This

Income Data	As a Pct of Net Sales
Net Sales (Gross Income)	100.00
Assets	
Cost of Sales	45.94
Gross Profit	53.03
Officer/Executive Salaries	0.0
Other General/Administrative Expenses	43.33
Operating Profit	7.00
Interest Expense	0.44
Depreciation	1.66
Profit before Taxes	2.43

Assets	Total Assets $50,000–$100,000	
Current Assets	As a Pct of Current Assets	As a Pct of Total Assets
Cash	8.14	3.74
Accounts Receivable	42.45	13.33
Inventories	25.18	17.54
Other Current Assets	0.21	0.18
Fixed Assets	As a Pct of Fixed Assets	As a Pct of Total Assets
Land, Buildings, Leasehold Improvements	30.58	10.09
Equipment	69.42	9.54
Other Fixed Assets	0.0	0.0

Liabilities & Capital		
Current Liabilities	As a Pct of Current Liabilities	As a Pct of Total Liabilities
Accounts Payable/Trade	41.98	14.41
Short Term Bank Loans	16.89	4.18
Other Current Debt	32.22	17.26
Long Term Debt	As a Pct of Long Term Debt	As a Pct of Total Liabilities
Mortgages Payable	0.0	0.0
Long Term Bank Loans	0.0	0.0
Stockholder Loans (Due to Owners)	0.0	0.0
Other Long Term Debt	0.0	0.0

Source: Financial Research Associates. Used with Permission.

Ratios	Median	Upper Quartile	Lower Quartile	Units
Current	2.4	6.3	1.2	Times
Quick	1.3	4.5	0.8	Times
Current Assets/Total Assets	45.9	78.5	25.8	Pct
Short Term Debt/Total Debt	57.4	82.2	24.7	Pct
Short Term Debt/Net Worth	32.6	130.5	6.5	Pct
Total Debt/Net Worth	102.9	225.7	5.9	Pct
Long Term Debt/Total Assets	16.1	38.7	6.8	Pct
Total Debt/Total Assets	56.4	83.5	7.6	Pct
Sales/Receivables	13.6	18.7	2.8	Times
Average Collection Period	22.0	28.0	1.0	Days
Sales/Inventory	18.0	32.1	11.8	Times
Sales/Total Assets	2.5	3.9	2.1	Times
Sales/Net Worth	4.2	14.8	2.5	Times
Profit (Pretax)/Total Assets	11.3	40.2	0.1	Pct
Profit (Pretax)/Net Worth	31.6	63.31	-11.6	Pct

FIGURE 6-4 RETAIL FLORIST STATEMENT STUDY

information is useful in establishing the asset commitments and performance characteristics of a "typical" firm in a particular business.

The source for the data in Figure 6-4 is *Financial Studies of the Small Business,* published annually by Financial Research Associates. Other sources of expense data that are oriented to the small firm are

- *Small Business Reporter*
  published by the Bank of America
- *Expenses in Retail Business*
  published by the National Cash Register Company

Sources oriented to larger firms but that may prove useful include

- *Statement Studies*
  published by Robert Morris Associates
- *Almanac of Business and Industrial Financial Ratios*
  by Leo Troy
- *Key Business Ratios*
  published by Dun and Bradstreet, Inc.

CONSTRUCTING SALES BUDGETS

Once the asset requirements and expenses have been estimated, the sales required to support the business can be determined.

The Breakeven Budget

Most managers have a notion of what level of sales is required to cover expenses. This can be thought of as an absolute dollar volume, units of product, or numbers of customers—whichever is most meaningful for a given business.

Formally, the zero profit point is termed the breakeven point. At this level of sales, all the expenses of the business are covered but there is no profit. In order to determine the breakeven point, an understanding of the cost-volume-profit relationships associated with the particular business operation is essential. *Fixed costs* are those expenses that do not vary with the level of sales activity. They generally include such expenses as rent, insurance, and management salaries, all of which are incurred regardless of sales activity. *Variable costs* are those that do vary directly with sales volume. The most common variable costs are direct material and labor in a manufacturing operation, or the cost of merchandise in a retail or wholesale firm.

In practice, the classification of costs as fixed or variable is not as straightforward as it may appear. A major determinant is the policies established by the business owners. For example, an advertising budget established for the near future can be treated as a fixed cost. On the other hand, if the budget is to be set as a percentage (say 2 percent) of sales volume, then advertising is essentially a variable expense. Remuneration of salespeople on a salary basis, straight commission, or base salary plus commission is also a decision that will affect the ratio of fixed to variable costs. The point is, some judgment is required to classify costs realistically.

Once the costs have been classified as either fixed or variable, the computation of a breakeven point is quite simple. The basic equation is

$$\text{Total Sales Revenue} = \text{Fixed Costs} + \text{Total Variable Costs}$$

which is equivalent to

$$\text{Price per Unit} \times \text{\# Units} = \text{Fixed Costs} + (\text{Variable Cost per Unit} \times \text{\# Units})$$

If this equation were solved for the number of units that needed to be sold in order to get to the zero profit point, the equation would look like this:

$$\frac{\text{Breakeven}}{\text{\# of units}} = \frac{\text{Fixed Costs}}{(\text{Selling Price} - \text{Variable Cost Per Unit})}$$

The denominator of the right-hand term (selling price – variable cost) is known as a *contribution margin*. It represents the amount of money left from the sale of a product that is available to contribute to paying fixed costs. For instance, if we buy shirts for $8 and sell them for $15, the contribution margin is $7 per shirt. Out of that $7 we must pay rent on the store, utilities, insurance, advertising, and other fixed expenses. For purposes of illustration, assume all fixed expenses at the shirt shop total $5000 per month. The breakeven point is the number of shirts that must be sold in order for that number of $7-per-shirt contribution margins to equal $5000 (the fixed costs):

$$\frac{\text{Breakeven}}{\text{\# of shirts}} = \frac{5000}{(15 - 8)}$$

$$\frac{\text{Breakeven}}{\text{\# of shirts}} = 715$$

Note that for each shirt sold past the 715-shirt breakeven point, the $7 contribution margin goes to the profit account. Consider the Dark Room to illustrate the expense schedules and the breakeven concept in a more realistic situation.

Case Study 6-1—The Dark Room

Alan Joyce was retiring from a university position as a photography instructor. He had extensive commercial-photography and film-processing experience prior to his teaching career. Alan had decided to open a do-it-yourself film-processing lab. The lab would offer fully equipped dark rooms for hourly rental fees.

Alan also planned to do some commercial film processing and to conduct classes in both photography and processing. He considered the classes as a way to develop customers for his rental darkrooms, and the commercial film processing was really a hobby that allowed him to keep in contact with his professional photographer friends. Neither of these activities was expected to contribute very much to revenues.

A 2000 sq. ft. facility has been leased at an annual rate of $6 per sq. ft. The proposed floor plan calls for two rental darkrooms, one teaching darkroom, one deluxe darkroom, a processing and finishing room, and a reception area. The fixed-asset and nonrecurring start-up expenses are given in Exhibits 6-1 and 6-2.

✓ Alan estimated the monthly operating expenses (Exhibit 6-3). He determined that he, personally, needed to draw $1000 a month from the business. He decided to hire a full-time clerical/receptionist person for $6.00/hr. Alan planned to employ students on a part-time basis to assist customers during the evening hours. He planned on 30 part-time hours per week at $3.50/hr.

Alan has planned a modest advertising program to promote his classes and darkroom facilities. His objective is to inform as many people as he can about the darkroom and to generate inquires about his classes and rentals. He has developed a media plan that includes a Yellow Pages listing, both the local and campus newspapers, and a cooperative direct-mail service. The display ad he plans for the hobby/craft section of the local newspaper is a biweekly expense; the direct-mail package to area households is bimonthly; and the campus newspaper ad is a monthly item. The total cost of the planned ads averages $400 per month (Exhibit 6-4).

By developing these schedules, Alan has identified the total capital required to start the Dark Room (15,705 + 4600 + 12,553 = 32,858). He plans to contribute about $13,000 of his own money and borrow the other $20,000. He has also identified the monthly operating expenses ($5328), which will be an important component in the sales budget computations.

As with most walk-in service businesses, most of the expenses Alan will face are fixed. Nonetheless, there are some judgment calls. (See Exhibit 6-5.)

Teaching Dark Room
Photo Equipment   *Per Unit*
  12 – Besseler 67C enlarger w/50 mm lens   193.95
   6 – Gra-Lab timers   63.98
  12 – Omega 8 × 10 borderless easels   13.95
     Misc. tongs, developing trays, safelights   200.00

Rental Darkrooms
   2 – Chromega B 600's with 2 lenses   595.90
   2 – Omega 4-in-1 easels   27.88
   2 – 8 × 10 color drums   28.00
   2 – 16 × 20 color drums   35.75
   2 – Gra-Lab timers   63.98
   2 – Motorized buses for color drums   60.00
   2 – 16 × 20 borderless easels   38.99
   2 – Contact proof printers   17.95
     Misc. tongs, developing trays   100.00

Deluxe Darkroom
   1 – Full set rental darkroom equipment   506.00
   1 – 4 × 5 enlarger color head   999.95

Processing, Drying, Mounting, and Finishing Room
   2 – Print dryers   100.00
   2 – Print washers   54.95
   4 – Weston thermometers   14.95
   1 – Kinderman film dryer   32.89
   2 – 7" tanks – 4 reels   26.50
   6 – 2" tanks – 1 reel   9.89
   3 – 3½" tanks – 2 reels   14.50
     Misc. clips, etc.   50.00

        TOTAL EQUIPMENT $7030.00

Office Equipment
   2 – Office desks   300.00
   2 – Desk chairs   120.00
  20 – Molded plastic chairs   38.00
   1 – 5 drawer filing cabinet   175.00
   4 – Reception area tables   100.00

       TOTAL OFFICE EQUIPMENT $ 2,175.00

LEASEHOLD IMPROVEMENTS $ 6,000.00
FIXTURES   500.00

TOTAL FIXED ASSETS REQUIRED $15,705.00

EXHIBIT 6-1   THE DARK ROOM FIXED ASSET REQUIREMENTS

Legal Fees	300.00
First and Last Month's Rent	2000.00
Office Supplies	500.00
Initial Film and Chemical Inventory	600.00
Initial Promotion Budget[1]	1000.00
Utility Deposits	200.00
TOTAL START-UP	$4600.00

[1] Flyers, display ads in students newspaper and local paper, Letter to area photographers

EXHIBIT 6-2   THE DARK ROOM
NONRECURRING START-UP EXPENSES

	Expenses	×	Months of Reserve	=	Capital Required
Rent	1000		3		3,000
Utilities	125		3		475
Telephone	75		3		225
Advertising	400		3		1,200
Owner's Draw	1000		1		1,000
Insurance	125		3		375
Payroll[1]	1380		3		4,140
Payroll Taxes and Fringes[2]	276		3		828
Supplies	200		1		200
Housekeeping	100		2		200
Sundry	50		2		100
Interest Expense[3]	270		3		810
Depreciation[4]	327		0		0
TOTAL EXPENSES	$5328				

TOTAL CAPITAL *(required to cover initial operating expenses)* $12,553

[1] 160 at 6.00/hour plus 120 at 3.50/hour
[2] Estimated at 20% of payroll
[3] Estimated as $20,000 principal at 16%
[4] 15705 ÷ 48 months straight line, 4-year life assumed

EXHIBIT 6-3   THE DARK ROOM
MONTHLY OPERATING EXPENSES

Medium	Monthly Cost
1 column × 1" Yellow Pages Ad	$ 33.50
2 column × 3" Display Ad in Hobby/Craft section, 2 Insertions/month @ $94	186.00
2 column × 3" Display Ad in campus newspaper, 2 Insertions/month @ $30.50	61.00
Cooperative Direct Mail Package, Bi-monthly — $240	120.00
	$400.50

EXHIBT 6-4 THE DARK ROOM
MONTHLY ADVERTISTING COSTS

Fixed	?	Variable
Rent	Utilities	Supplies
Telephone	Payroll	
Advertising	Payroll Tax and Fringes	
Owner's Draw	Housekeeping	
Insurance	Sundry	
Interest Expenses		
Depreciation		

EXHIBIT 6-5 THE DARK ROOM
COST CLASSIFICATIONS

Alan realizes that in order to estimate the breakeven point he must classify the expenses in the center ("?") column as either fixed or variable. Utilities, housekeeping, and sundry expenses will vary to some extent with the usage of the rental darkrooms—but they will not be zero if there are no rental customers. That is, each of these costs have fixed *and* variable components. Because these are minor monthly expenses, and to err on the side of conservatism, he decides to treat them as fixed. Payroll and payroll taxes also have fixed and variable components. The full-time clerical/receptionist will be necessary regardless of rental activity, but the part-time student help will only be scheduled if rental activity warrants it. Therefore he decides to classify the clerical salary and payroll taxes as fixed (160 × $6.00/hr × 1.20) and the part-time payroll as variable (120 × $3.50/hr × 1.20).

Supplies for the dark rooms constitutes the only "true" variable expense. Alan estimates that about $1.00 worth of chemicals and solutions will be consumed during the average rental hour. Alan plans to be open 12 hours per day (9 a.m. to 9 p.m.), six days a week, or a total of 288 hours per month. For the two rental darkrooms, the total rental hours available per month is 576. The hourly rate for part-time help is $504/576 or about $0.88 per hour. Total variable cost per rental hour is therefore $1.88.

By establishing a rental rate per hour, Alan can compute the breakeven point:

$$
\begin{aligned}
\text{Sales Revenue} &= \text{Fixed Expenses} + \text{Variable Expenses} \\
\$25 \times \text{\# of hours} &= 4624 + (1.88 \times \text{\# of hours}) \\
23.12 \times \text{\# of hours} &= 4624 \\
\text{\# of hours} &= 4624/23.12 \\
\text{\# of hours} &= 200
\end{aligned}
$$

The breakeven point is 200 rental hours per month at $25 per hour rental fee. That converts to a breakeven dollar volume of $5200. In other words, Alan must operate at 35 percent of capacity (200/576 possible hours) in order to break even on the rental business.

The breakeven analysis can also be depicted graphically, as in Exhibit 6-6. While a bit more cumbersome, the cost-volume-profit relationships are more apparent.

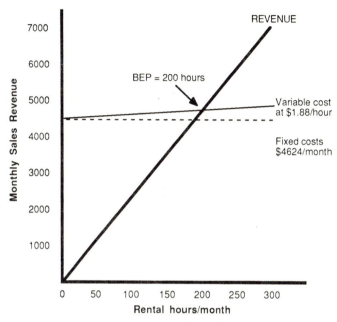

**EXHIBIT 6-6 THE DARK ROOM
BREAKEVEN ANALYSIS**

Cost-of-Capital Sales Budget

At the breakeven level, the firm can meet its short-term obligations to suppliers, landlords, and employees. However, the obligations to the owners and the suppliers of capital are not being met at this level of operations. The firm, therefore, is not viable at this sales volume. The owners, receiving no return on their capital, will eventually withdraw and reinvest their funds somewhere else. The purpose of deriving the cost-of-capital sales budget is to determine the sales volume necessary to compensate the owners for the use of their money.

Determining the rate of return a business should earn on the capital invested is not a simple issue. Indeed, much of modern financial theory is devoted to estimating the cost of capital in various business ventures.

At the very least, the owners should earn what has been termed the "risk-free" rate of return. As the term implies, this is the return earned on funds invested in very stable, or risk-less, investments. In practice, the "risk-free" rate is generally regarded as the rate paid on investments in government securities. Bonds issued by the U.S. Treasury are backed by the federal government: they are "risk-free" in the sense that the probability of default is negligible.

Investors in business ventures always face the possibility of losing all or part of their money should the venture fail. Therefore, they are entitled to a risk premium over and above the risk-free return. In theory, the risk premium is equivalent to the return earned in excess of the risk- free rate in similar business ventures.

But when you're considering small business ventures, what businesses are similar? In reality, the risk premium is affected by what the investors believe they can earn in alternative investments. Rates of return in the 20–30 percent range are realistic expectations. For planning purposes, the interest rate on borrowed funds can be thought as the minimum rate that investors should earn.

By adding a return on the money Alan Joyce will invest in the Dark Room, the cost-of-capital sales budget can be derived. Alan has arranged to borrow $20,000 from a commercial bank at 16 percent interest. He has incorporated the monthly interest expense as an operating expense in the breakeven sales budget. In addition to the borrowed money, Alan plans to contribute $13,000 of his own money to the venture. He has derived several different sales budgets (see Exhibit 6-7) reflecting different rates of return on his $13,000.

The return on his invested capital represents an increase in his fixed operating expenses. From the analysis in Exhibit 6-7, Alan can see that he must rent his darkrooms at least 36 percent of the available hours to earn a reasonable return on his $13,000.

	16%	*20%*	*25%*
Fixed Operating Expenses	4624	4624	4624
Plus Return on Owner's Investment	174	217	271
Total Fixed Expenses	4798	4841	4895
Rental Hours Required[1]	208	210	212
Sales Level Required $5400	5200	5250	5300
Percent of Capacity[2]	36.0	36.5	37.0

[1] Total Fixed Expenss/(hourly rental of $25 – variable cost of $1.88/hour)
[2] Rental hours required/576 maximum possible hours

EXHIBIT 6-7   THE DARK ROOM
MONTHLY COST-OF-CAPITAL SALES BUDGETS

Chapter 7

Developing a
Realistic Forecast

A realistic sales forecast is one that is consistent with both the facts of the marketplace and the cost structure of the business venture. The previous chapters have dealt with the estimation of total market potential and with the determination of sales volume requirements for survival and profitability. Armed with these facts, the task of merging them and constructing a sensible forecast can be approached.

INITIAL COMPARISONS

The share of the existing market required to break even and cover the cost of capital are the first computations to perform. Curiosity would have motivated most people to figure these in their head by this point in the analysis. The required market penetration for survival is an initial test of the feasibility of the venture. Of course, the lower the required share the better.

If these initial computations indicate that substantial proportions of the existing market must be served to survive, the feasibility of the venture must be questioned. This is the first recursive "loop" in the MP-SR procedure. If a 50 percent market share will be necessary for the venture to survive, it's time to reconsider some of the basic premises on which this venture was conceived.

Revision of the initial plan can focus on several different areas. First, with respect to the estimated market potential:

- *Redefine the trade area.* Has the trade area been defined too conservatively? Can changes in the promotional campaign or the location permit access to a larger group of prospective customers?
- *Reconsider the revenue per customer.* Is the initial pricing plan unnecessarily low? Can revenue per customer be increased through price modifications, cross-selling of additional products or services, or service extensions such as delivery, repair services, or credit terms?
- *Reconsider the product/service mix.* Are there other customers that can be served? This is really a revision of the original target market definition. If the assets of the venture can be used to generate alternative streams of revenue, required market penetration can be reduced.

A second area for possible revisions is, of course, the sales requirements. Here, approaches to lowering the breakeven point must be considered.

- *Reduction of asset requirements.* Can the expenses associated with fixed assets be reduced? Are planned leasehold improvements unnecessarily extravagant?
- *Reduce operating expenses.* Are the management salaries and fringes too generous? Can materials, merchandise and labor costs be reduced? Are the planned promotional budget and other selling expenses excessive?

Revisions based on these questions will require reworking the market potential side of the forecasting procedure and/or the sales requirements side. It is foolish, however, to proceed until a conceivable level of market penetration can be envisioned. If no revisions can be justified in the original plan, serious consideration should be given to abandoning the venture idea.

JUDGING LIKELY SALES GROWTH

Once a plan has been judged feasible in terms of the required share of the market, the rate of market penetration, or sales growth, can be examined. Sales growth enjoyed by a new venture or a new product line is a function of three factors:

- The number and behavior of existing competitors
- Sources of competitive advantage
- Overall market growth

The appraisal of these factors requires judgment and the ability to project oneself into the positions of a competitor and a customer. Questions such as "How would I react to a new competitor in my market?" and "As a customer, why would I do business with a particular firm?" must be answered realistically.

Evaluating Existing Competitors

Competitors came in two forms: direct and indirect. Direct competitors are those businesses that offer products and services similar to those under consideration. Indirect competitors are those offering products or services that are dissimilar but are substitutes in that they satisfy the same customer needs. Home nursing services are indirect competitors with nursing homes and hardware stores that rent rug-cleaning equipment are indirect competitors with carpet cleaning services.

In analyzing indirect competitors, the principal concern is their growth. Rapid acceptance and expansion of what are considered indirect competitors indicates consumer acceptance of the substitute good or service. At some point, these indirect competitors must be treated as direct competitors. Already movie theater operators are directly competing with video-rental outlets and pay-TV subscription services for family recreation expenditures, and service station operators are competing with convenience stores and specialized oil-change and tune-up outlets. It is important to remember that markets are defined not by purveyors of goods and services but by consumers.

In evaluating direct competitors and principal indirect competitors it is useful to gather and organize data on each competitor. Once collected, this information can assist us in drawing inferences about likely acceptance and competitive reactions. Questions to be raised:

- Who are the principal competitors in this market and what reputation, goodwill, and loyalty do they enjoy?
- Has the number of competitors changed in recent years? What are the characteristics of new entrants? Which competitors have withdrawn from the market?
- How similar are the product lines of these competitors?
- What services are offered during and after the sale? Which of these seem important to customers?
- How aggressive are the managers of these competitors? Do they engage in intense promotion and selling efforts? Have they introduced new product lines recently, or have they expanded facilities or locations?
- Do these competitors have access to capital, either by virtue of a solid balance sheet or a corporate parent?
- How important is this particular line of business to each competitor? Is it their "bread and butter" or a minor source of revenue and profit?
- How did the existing competitors react to recent entrants? Did they cut prices or raise legal challenges?

Sources of Competitive Advantage

Eventually in the planning of any business venture the crucial question "Why will anyone buy from me?" must be answered. In some rare instances customers patronize a business because they have no alternative. Being the only supplier of a product or service to a particular market can be an attractive situation. However, monopoly power tends to be short-lived. If the business is successful, others will be attracted and eventually enter. Even protected monopolies face patent expiration or some form of public regulation. By and large, to be successful firms must enjoy some form of competitive advantage.

Common sources of competitive advantage in small firms include

- **Location** providing greater convenience to customers, reduced transportation costs, lower operating expenses, or better visibility and traffic flow
- **Specialization** reflected in the depth of product lines and the sophistication and knowledge of sales personnel
- **Product line breadth and exclusivity** resulting from protected distributor relationships and/or multiple vendors and broad inventory holdings
- **After-sale support** in terms of warranty, repair and service, delivery, installation, and floor-plan financing
- **Cost position** resulting from more efficient production, more favorable supply terms, lower overhead expenses, or avowed "meet the competition" pricing
- **Channels of distribution** that are unique in that they offer cost savings (e.g., factory outlet) or customer convenience (e.g., shop-at-home, mail-order)
- **Product quality** due to exacting production standards, superior raw materials, or careful selection of brand name manufacturers as vendors
- **Customer base** representing established long-term relationships with loyal purchasers. This is particularly valuable in product line additions where cross-selling is important

The use of a source, or combination of sources, of competitive advantage serves to define the position that the venture will seek to occupy in the market. A viable position will emphasize advantages that are important to the target consumer's purchase decision and will not be easily copied by existing competitors.

Market Growth

Growth in total market demand is a generally favorable condition that has several important implications for judging likely sales growth. Observed and anticipated growth in demand is the result of any one factor or some combination of several factors:

- Population growth in the trade area (e.g., branch banks, supermarkets)
- Improved purchasing power in the trade area (e.g., restaurants, specialty clothing stores)
- Changes in the way consumers seek to satisfy existing needs due to changes in technology or distribution methods (e.g., VCR's, microwave ovens, outpatient surgery centers, 10-minute oil changes)
- Changes in the needs that consumers seek to satisfy (e.g., exercise equipment and apparel, day-care centers)

Understanding which of these forces is operating in a particular market can provide insights into the most salient forms of competitive advantage. For example, growth spurred by increasing purchasing power is frequently associated with emergence of convenience-based ventures, and those that emphasize improved product or service quality.

Irrespective of the underlying causes of market growth, operating in a growth market has two important implications for sales forecasting. First, if growth cannot be served by existing competitors, the ready acceptance of a new entrant is more likely. If the appropriate sources of competitive advantage are employed, sales growth in the initial months can be substantial. In slow growth markets or in markets where existing competitors can easily satisfy demand growth, the rate of penetration is likely to be slower.

Second, entry into a growing market is less likely to elicit strong reactions by existing competitors. Promotional activities and discounting to block entry are far more likely in stagnant markets where any success enjoyed by the new entrant is at the expense of existing competitors.

PREPARING THE FORECASTS

How many months will it take to reach a breakeven level of operations? Having thought through the complexities of the market, planned competitive position, and cost structure, this central question can now be addressed. The preceding analysis should permit the formulation of some reasonable assumptions regarding sales penetration. However, because any assumption must embody some degree of uncertainty, it is advisable to formulate several sets of assumptions. In order to bracket likely market acceptance, it is useful to develop favorable and unfavorable scenarios (see Figure 7-1).

Factors to be considered include:

- *The degree of customer acceptance* based on loyalty to existing competitors
- *Salience of competitive advantages,* such as price or quality, in motivating purchase behavior
- *Ability to defend and preserve sources of competitive advantage*
- *Likely competitive reaction* to entry, such as discounting and promotion efforts
- *Anticipated market growth*

Forecasting Scenarios

	Optimistic	*Most Likely*	Pessimistic
Degree of Customer Acceptance	Substantial——▶	◀————	Limited
Salience of Competitive Advantages	High———————▶	◀————	Low
Ability to Preserve Competitive Advantages	Strong———▶	◀————	Weak
Competitive Reaction to Entry	Benign———▶	◀————	Intense
Anticipated Market Growth	Rapid———————▶	◀———	Stagnant

FIGURE 7-1   ASSUMPTIONS FOR SCENARIO DEVELOPMENT

Case Study 7-1—The Dark Room (continued)

Alan Joyce was disturbed by the cost analysis discussed in Chapter 6. That analysis indicated that he must rent 36 percent of his available darkroom hours in order to break even and earn a minimal return on his invested money.

Although the trade area encompasses over 200,000 residents and there are no existing darkroom rental facilities, Alan is unsure about how many serious amateur photographers there are. Indeed, it is the serious hobbyist who is Alan's primary target market. In an effort to lower the planned breakeven point, Alan reexamined his operating costs and concluded that it was unreasonable to think they could be reduced. Alan then turned his attention to the revenue side of his planned venture. The trade area couldn't be amended, because it currently included the entire community. Similarly, Alan believed the initial pricing at $25 per hour could not be raised. Eventually, Alan realized that he must expand the service mix of the Dark Room in order to lower the number of rental hours necessary to break even.

Alan had originally planned to perform some commercial photography work and had equipped the deluxe darkroom for that purpose. Alan had also designed and planned to equip a teaching darkroom so that he could eventually hold classes for people interested in learning photography techniques. Although he had hoped the revenue from these services would not be necessary for the survival of the venture, he now realized that it was. Alan set out to develop a sales forecast for each of his three services—darkroom rentals, photography classes, and commercial photography.

Darkroom Rentals

As the "backbone" of proposed venture, the rental business is the one that Alan had considered most thoroughly. There are no direct competitors in the trade area. While there are a number of film processing businesses, the only alternative for a person interested in processing and printing his or her own film is to equip a darkroom at home. This is an expensive proposition in terms of space and equipment, and is likely to appeal to only the most ardent photography buffs.

Relatively inexpensive kits for home developing are available from several area mass merchandisers. These kits, however, are intended for youngsters in the same way that chemistry sets and microscope kits are sold. Alan doesn't consider these to have any influence on his target market.

The principal competitive advantage the rental business would enjoy is, of course, uniqueness. Alan feels that the quality of equipment and facilities and the availability of advice from either himself or his part-time employees will also be important to his rental patrons.

Market growth is favorable in terms of population growth in the trade area (10 percent annual population growth in recent years) and increased interest in do-it-yourself hobby activities in general, and photography in particular.

Photography Classes

Within the trade area a public and a private university each offer courses in photography and film processing. The private university restricts enrollment to its own students. The public university is Alan's employer and permits both students and nonstudents to enroll through its continuing education programs. The courses meet on a regular basis for the fall semester and are inexpensive ($50). Alan believes this is his major competitor in the education market.

The university's reputation for teaching these courses is pretty good. The facilities are adequate and the instruction is competent—Alan himself has taught these courses. Complaints from students concern the size of the classes (usually 30 people) and the spreading of class sessions over an entire semester (about 4 months). Alan thinks he can achieve a competitive advantage by offering shorter, more concentrated courses and by restricting his class size to 12 students. Further, the university is unlikely to respond to the opening of the Dark Room. The revenue generated from the photography courses is not significant in terms of the university budget. Alan knows the institution to be quite inflexible about its scheduling and registration procedures. He concludes that even if the university were so inclined, it might be unable to respond to his entry into the market.

Market growth for photography and film-processing instruction enjoys the same favorable trends as the rental business. Alan is privy to the enrollment data at the university, which are a direct indication of the market trends. The university courses are quite popular and have grown both in size and number in recent semesters.

Commercial Photography

There are presently 32 commercial photography studios within the trade area. Of these competitors, 8 offer very limited services—such as passport photos or graphic slides—but the remaining 24 are full-service commercial studios. Alan has been involved in this market as a free-lancer for several years, and he has developed some contacts with commercial printers and advertising agencies that make extensive use of photographic services. However, a number of the existing studios are well entrenched in the market. Several have been in existence for over fifteen years and have developed relationships with the major consumers of commercial services.

Alan also realizes that he can offer no particular competitive advantage. His equipment and skills are not unique. If he tries to underprice his services, he may be hired for some projects, but eventually other photographers will do the same. Besides, the market is presently competitive and prices are not out of line with similar services in other markets that Alan is familiar with.

Overall, Alan is hesitant to rely on this market as a major source of revenue.

The Forecasts

Alan has formulated an optimistic, pessimistic, and likely set of assumptions for each his three services. These assumptions reflect different levels of customer acceptance, competitive advantage, and market growth over the first year of operations (see Exhibit 7-1).

Darkroom rentals   Growth in rental hours per month is
the major variable for forecasting this revenue stream. Among
Alan's friends and former students, he is confident that 50
hours per month will be rented. Optimistically, he assumes
that his advertising, word-of-mouth among his friends, associates, and the people in his classes will result in the addition of 15 hours per month during year 1 (about 30 percent
growth). Pessimistically, Alan assumes that only his friends
and former students will rent darkrooms for the first 3 months,
and growth of 5 hours per month is experienced after that (10
percent growth). The likely case is based on level sales for
months 1 and 2 followed by several months of 15 percent
growth increasing to 20 percent growth for the second half of
year 1.

						Months						
	1	2	3	4	5	6	7	8	9	10	11	12
Optimistic *(30% Growth)*												
Hours/Month	50	65	80	95	110	125	140	155	170	185	200	215
Revenue	$1250	1625	2000	2375	2750	3125	3500	3875	4250	4625	5000	5375
Likely *(16–20% Growth)*												
Hours/Month	50	50	58	66	74	82	92	102	112	122	132	142
Revenue	$1250	1250	1450	1650	1850	2050	2300	2550	2800	3050	3300	3550
Pessimistic *(10% Growth)*												
Hours/Month	50	50	50	55	60	65	70	75	80	85	90	95
Revenue	$1250	1250	1250	1375	1500	1625	1750	1875	2000	2125	2250	2375

**EXHIBIT 7-1   GROWTH SCENARIOS FOR
THE DARK ROOM RENTAL BUSINESS**

Photography classes   Alan plans to offer courses of four
weeks' duration, commencing on the first of every month. Students will enroll in one of three classes: two evenings per week

for 90-minute sessions, two days per week for 90-minute sessions, or Saturday mornings for a 3-hour session. Maximum enrollment for each class is 12 students. Alan feels it is necessary to offer the courses for the same $50 fee as the university offers. Optimistically, he forecasts a total enrollment of 15 (averaging 5 students per class) in the early months, with gradual growth to full capacity of 36 students by the end of year 1. Pessimistically, Alan feels that enrollments of at least 2 students per course in the early months is a minimum. He further anticipates gradual growth to two thirds of capacity (8 students per class) by the end of year 1. The likely scenario, of course, falls between the pessimistic and optimistic outlooks. (Exhibit 7-2).

					Months							
	1	2	3	4	5	6	7	8	9	10	11	12
Optimistic												
Total Enrollment	15	15	17	19	21	23	25	27	30	32	34	36
Revenue	$750	750	850	950	1050	1150	1250	1350	1500	1600	1700	1800
Likely												
Total Enrollment	6	8	10	12	14	16	18	20	22	24	26	28
Revenue	$300	400	500	600	700	800	900	1000	1100	1200	1300	1400
Pessimistic												
Total Enrollment	6	6	6	8	10	12	14	16	18	20	22	24
Revenue	$300	300	300	400	500	600	700	800	900	1000	1100	1200

**EXHIBIT 7-2   GROWTH SCENARIOS FOR
THE PHOTOGRAPHY CLASS BUSINESS**

Commercial photography   As a free-lance photographer, Alan presently bills about $4000 a year. This represents work that he fits into his current teaching schedule. Because he has no real competitive advantage, his pessimistic outlook is that he will merely continue doing about the same amount of commercial work. This would average $350 per month. Alan does, however, feel that there are other jobs he could get from his existing contacts if he expressed that interest to them and informed them of his less restricted schedule. He believes it is likely he could double his billings during the first year. Thinking as optimistically as possible about the growth of the businesses in which he has contacts he can foresee a chance that he could triple his commercial billings (Exhibit 7-3).

						Months						
	1	2	3	4	5	6	7	8	9	10	11	12
Optimistic (3 × Current Billings)												
Revenue	$350	350	450	550	650	750	850	950	1050	1050	1050	1050
Likely (2 × Current Billings)												
Revenue	$350	350	450	450	550	550	700	700	700	700	700	700
Pessimistic (Maintain Current Billings)												
Revenue	$350	350	350	350	350	350	350	350	350	350	350	350

EXHIBIT 7-3   GROWTH SCENARIOS FOR THE COMMERCIAL PHOTOGRAPHY BUSINESS

The Composite Forecast

Once the forecasts for each line of business are complete, a composite sales forecast can be prepared.

The composite forecast indicates that under Alan's optimistic assumptions, the Dark Room would break even and cover the cost of invested capital at the end of month 7. The most likely revenue streams indicate a breakeven during month 12. Only under the pessimistic assumption would the venture still be losing money after a year of operations (Exhibit 7-4).

		Months									
1	*2*	*3*	*4*	*5*	*6*	*7*	*8*	*9*	*10*	*11*	*12*

Optimistic

	1	2	3	4	5	6	7	8	9	10	11	12
Rentals	1250	1625	2000	2375	2750	3125	3500	3875	4250	4625	5000	5375
Classes	750	750	850	950	1050	1150	1250	1350	1500	1600	1700	1800
Comm.	350	350	450	550	650	750	850	950	1050	1050	1050	1050
Total Revenue	$2350	2725	3300	3875	4450	5025	5600*	6175	6800	7275	7750	8225

Likely

	1	2	3	4	5	6	7	8	9	10	11	12
Rentals	1250	1250	1450	1650	1850	2050	2300	2550	2800	3050	3300	3550
Classes	300	400	500	600	700	800	900	1000	1100	1200	1300	1400
Comm.	350	350	450	450	550	550	700	700	700	700	700	700
Total Revenue	$1900	2000	2400	2700	3100	3400	3900	4250	4600	4950	5300	5650*

Pessimistic

	1	2	3	4	5	6	7	8	9	10	11	12
Rentals	1250	1250	1250	1375	1500	1625	1750	1875	2000	2125	2250	2375
Classes	300	300	300	400	500	600	700	800	900	1000	1100	1200
Comm.	350	350	350	350	350	350	350	350	350	350	350	350
Total Revenue	$1900	1900	1900	2125	2350	2575	2800	3025	3250	3475	3700	3925

*Month in which revenue exceeds 25% cost-of-capital sales budget of $5500.

EXHIBIT 7-4   COMPOSITE SALES FORECAST FOR YEAR 1

Chapter 8

Sales Forecasting as a Management Control Tool

Throughout this book we've viewed the process of forecasting as a planning activity. New venture feasibility and geographic expansion possibilities have been assessed on the basis of planned sales and planned expenses. It is important, in this final chapter, to recognize the crucial role forecasting plays in the process of management control.

MANAGEMENT CONTROL

A supervisor observing the way a salesperson handles an inquiry and then making suggestions on how his or her response might be improved is a form of management control. Standards established for the quality of inputs and policies that govern the granting of credit to customers are also control practices. The basic control activities in business organizations focus on controlling the quantity and quality of resources, the actual performance of work, and monitoring performance.

The objective of any control effort is to ensure that resources available to the business are being used effectively. The general control process is depicted in Figure 8-1. The process requires standards to which performance can be compared and information on current performance. The comparison, if unsatisfactory, should instigate corrective action. Corrective actions can involve changes in resources, either quantity or quality, changes in the allocation of existing resources, changes in work activities, or changes in existing standards.

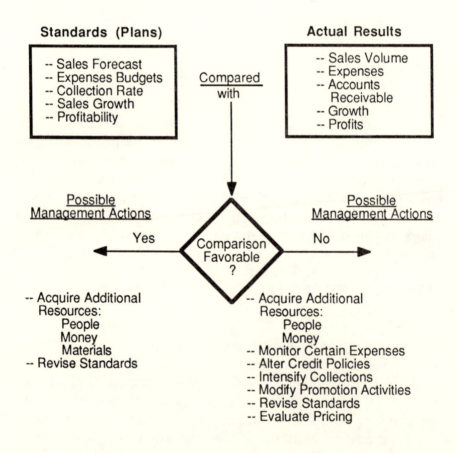

FIGURE 8-1   MANAGEMENT CONTROL PROCESS

Sales forecasts and expense forecasts contribute to the control process by creating the standards to which results are compared. The periodic comparison of actual results to planned expenses and sales serves several functions.

First, it serves a score-keeping function that enables us to see how we're doing. Were our assumptions about the market, our competitors, our labor and material costs correct?

Second, comparisons of actual and planned results serve to focus attention. When sizable deviations appear, either favorable or unfavorable, some management action is called for. For instance, if cash received is running behind projections, changes in credit terms or intensified collection efforts may be instituted as corrective action. Favorable deviations, such as sales volume exceeding the forecast, also require management attention. Supply orders and working capital arrangements for the financing of inventories and receivables are likely to be altered under these welcome circumstances.

Third, forecast and result comparisons serve to sharpen forecasting skills. Underestimated expenses, hidden costs, or previously unknown seasonal sales fluctuations can be identified and incorporated into future forecasts.

The main point is that the ability to exercise management control is made possible by the previous planning activity. The process of formulating forecasts results not only in a plan but also in a powerful control device.

The Control Cycle

The control problem is an ongoing one in a business venture. Control activities are best implemented as a cyclical process in which periods of business activity are compared to plans and corrective actions are taken.

Determining the time period in which the cycle should operate—daily, weekly, monthly, quarterly or annually—is problematic. The IRS imposes at least an annual review of revenue and expenses for tax purposes. While an annual cycle is useful for reporting to outsiders such as banks and outside owners, it is inadequate for control purposes. To monitor results and institute timely corrective action, the cycle should span no more than a quarter. In most businesses a monthly cycle is optimal.

This is not meant to imply that all control activities should operate on a monthly cycle. In retail businesses the reconciliation of cash with register receipts is performed daily. Performance evaluations of employees, an important control activity, is best handled on semi-annually or annually. The monthly control cycle advocated here is appropriate for the comparison of sales and expense forecasts to actual results.

Variance Analysis

The "tool" for detecting deviations from planned activities is, in accounting jargon, known as variance analysis. Consider Figure 8-2, which is based on a standard profit-and-loss statement format.

The *forecast* column is completed directly from the sales and expense forecasts we've been discussing throughout the last three chapters. The *actual* column is completed from the operating results over the same one-month period. The *variance* column is simply the difference between the forecast and actual amounts. Unfavorable variances are generally depicted in parentheses ( ). (Keep in mind that the direction of unfavorable variances differs in sales and expense categories. Sales shortfalls are unfavorable while expense shortfalls usually are not.)

The first three columns are straightforward. The *volume adjusted* column requires some explanation. In the event that there is a sales volume variance, forecasted amounts in variable cost categories will not be relevant for variance analysis. The purpose of volume adjustments is to estimate what varia-

Month _____

Revenue	Forecast	Actual	Variance	Volume Adjusted
Cash Sales				
Sales on Account				
Receivables Collected				
Expenses				
Cost of Goods				
Labor				
Rent				
Advertising				
Suppliers				
Legal/Acctg.				
Utilities				
Phone				
Sales Commissions				
Sundry				
TOTAL EXPENSES	_____	_____	_____	_____
Operating Profit				

FIGURE 8-2   MONTHLY VARIANCE WORKSHEET

ble expenses should have been given the actual level of sales activity. For example, recall the cost structure of the Emergency Medical Center. EMC costs for malpractice insurance and supplies vary directly with the number of patient visits. The forecasted amount for those expenses must therefore be based on the sales forecast. If the forecasted sales base is not achieved (unfavorable variance), it makes little sense to compare actual supply and insurance expenses with their respective forecasts. Volume adjustments are made to determine what insurance costs and supply costs should have been at the achieved level of sales.

In order to illustrate the use of variance analysis, reconsider the Floral Supply case study from Chapter 5.

Case Study 8-1—The Floral Supply (continued)

After Regina and Charles had estimated the market potential of the retail florist under new management, they established a vendor relationship with the new owners and encouraged them to develop their retail market.

The new owners prepared sales and expense forecasts based on the historical records of the previous owners and the changes they were planning to make in the operation of the store. The changes included an expanded delivery service and a more aggressive advertising program.

They developed a control system based on a monthly cycle and used variance analysis to detect problems and to develop a better understanding of the business. (See Exhibit 8-1.)

The results for the month of July were somewhat disappointing. Sales revenue was not as high as they had hoped, and operating profit was more than $3000 less than forecast. Initially, the new owners realized that a good portion of the profit variance is a function of the low sales volume. They also realize that there is not much, as retailers, that they can do about month-to-month fluctuations. Even though sales were low, the total expenses varied unfavorably with the forecast by $411. This really isn't much money, and if sales had hit the forecast they would have ignored it. However, when they adjusted the variances to reflect the actual sales volume of $27,214, the picture looked far worse. Three large unfavorable variances are obvious.

Cost of Goods   The favorable variance of $538 becomes an $816 unfavorable variance when adjusted for sales volume. Cost of goods has traditionally run at 45 percent of sales, which means the expense should have been $12,246 (.45 × 27,214) at the actual sales level. The owners concede that they had

	July			Volume Adjusted Variances
	Forecast	Actual	Variance	
Sales	30,000	27,214	(2,786)	
Cash Received	31,575	30,082	(1,493)	
Account Receivable Balance	22,600	21,415	1,185	
Expenses				
Cost of Goods *(45%)	13,600	13,062	538	(816)
Rent	2,300	2,300	0	0
Utilities	450	417	33	33
Telephone	200	212	(12)	(12)
Advertising	2,800	3,600	(800)	(800)
Insurance	110	110	0	0
Payroll & Taxes *(9.7%)	2,900	3,140	(240)	(500)
Delivery Van Lease	310	310	0	0
Van Expenses *(1.1%)	325	282	43	17
Office Supplies	75	143	(68)	(68)
Shop Supplies *(.7%)	200	194	6	(4)
Owner's Draw	1,200	1,200	0	0
Sundry *(.8%)	250	161	89	56
Total Expenses	24,720	25,131	(411)	(2,094)
Operating Profit	5,280	2,083	(3,197)	

*Variable Cost—( )—is percent of sales revenue

**EXHIBIT 8-1   MONTHLY VARIANCE ANALYSIS
THE FLORAL SUPPLY**

become lax in preparing orders and had delegated the ordering of some standard items to an employee. Overordering of some items had resulted in spoilage and the need to mark down some items. They recognized the importance of this function and intend to be more thoughtful about procurement in the future.

Advertising   The ad budget was not a function of current sales. It was, in effect, a fixed cost once they had committed to media space and time contracts. The variance of $800 is the result of production costs for two new radio commercials their ad agency had prepared. This is a one-time cost that was not anticipated in the forecast, but which they feel is justified and will pay off in the future.

Payroll   Labor expenses are partially a function of sales activity. For control purposes they treat it as a straight variable expense. Much of the unfavorable variance of $500 is due to overtime paid to a key employee who had to stay beyond her scheduled hours due to evening store traffic. They feel that through more careful scheduling of work hours and by shifting some of the daytime hours to the evening schedule, this expense can be avoided in the future.

The other variances, favorable and unfavorable, are trivial and not worth worrying about. However, from their analysis, they believed that by controlling ordering and work schedules better, they probably could have made an additional $1000 in July.

USING A CONTINUOUS FORECAST

In practice, the use of forecasting as a planning and control tool can best be achieved by creating a continuous forecast. The concept behind a continuous forecast is that, once a venture is in operation, the forecast should periodically be extended into the future. The extension blends judgments about future demand, competition, and market growth along with recent operating experiences. For instance, a one-year forecast has been advocated in this book at the start of a new venture. Once in operation, variance analysis and control can be exercised at monthly intervals. At the end of the first quarter of operations, the forecast is "pushed" into the future one quarter. In other words, a forecast one year into the future is always current. (See Figure 8-3.)

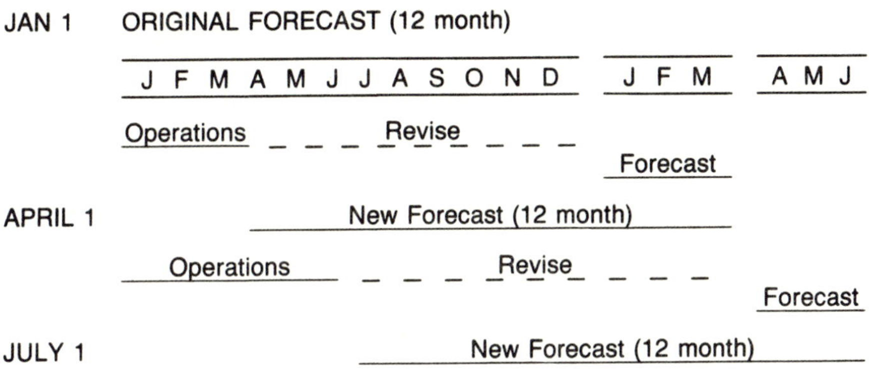

JAN 1   ORIGINAL FORECAST (12 month)

| J F M A M J J A S O N D | J F M | A M J |

Operations _ _ _ Revise _ _ _

Forecast

APRIL 1   New Forecast (12 month)

Operations   _ _ _ Revise _ _ _

Forecast

JULY 1   New Forecast (12 month)

FIGURE 8-3   A CONTINUOUS FORECASTING CYCLE

A continuous forecasting process allows the most recent operating experience to be incorporated in the plans for the immediate future. It serves to detect and rationalize the need for developing future resources such as physical space, labor, and capital. Over time, the continuous forecast can also incorporate known seasonal fluctuations, and may eventually lead to the use of the more sophisticated data-based forecasting techniques. Most important, the continuous forecast requires a disciplined approach to thinking about the customer, the market, and the future of the business. While we all acknowledge that periodic reflection and planning is beneficial, in the midst of day-to-day operations and ''fire-fighting'' those activities are often neglected.

Appendix A

Secondary Data Sources

The following data sources have been organized into four major categories:

1. Government publications
2. Commercial services
3. Trade associations
4. Index services

While most of these data are available for individual purchase, the most economical source is through the public library or the closest university library. Inquire at the Reference section or Government Documents section of the library to determine if the source you seek is part of the library's holdings or if the library can secure it for you.

This list is not exhaustive, but it does contain the most useful sources of data for our purposes.

GOVERNMENT PUBLICATIONS

Census Data (Government Documents or Reference Section)

Census of Population Population, age distributions, income distributions, education, school enrollment, family size and structure, occupation, and a variety of other demographic and sociological data. Breakdowns by state, county, municipality, and standard metropolitan statistical area (SMSA).

Census of Housing   Detailed analysis of housing stock, including age of structure, owner/renter-occupied, number of bedrooms and baths, plumbing fixtures, heating source, source of water, tenure, rental costs, mortgage status, vehicles available, and so on. Breakdowns by counties and size of town.

Census of Population and Housing   Selected data from the population and housing analysis broken down to census tract units. Census tracts are geographic divisions bounded by streets or other visible boundaries. They are intended to be homogeneous with respect to economic conditions and generally contain between 2500 and 8000 people. Due to growth in certain areas, tract boundaries are sometimes redefined, creating some difficulties in comparability over time.

Census of Retail Trade   Number of establishments, sales volume, and payroll data by type of retail store (e.g., eating and drinking places, apparel and accessory shops). Breakdowns by SMSA and census defined Central Business Districts (CBD's).

Census of Wholesale Trade   Similar data by type of wholesale business. Major breakdowns into durable and nondurable goods, with subdivisions by line of business (e.g., grocery and related products, paper and paper products). Geographic breaks by SMSA and size of business district (i.e., number of establishments).

Census of Service Industries   Similar data by service type (e.g., hotel/motel, personal services, business services, automotive). Similar geographic breaks.

Other censuses that may prove useful in particular circumstances include:

Census of Manufacturers
Census of Transportation
Census of Mineral Industries
Census of Agriculture

County Business Patterns

Contains employment, payroll, and the number of establishments broken down by employment size (e.g., 1–4 employees, 5–9 employees, etc.). Industry breakdowns similar to the retail, wholesale, and service industry census. Geographic breakdowns by state and county.

Small Business Administration

The SBA publishes a variety of information on small business practices and common decision situations. Some libraries may hold the following publications. Otherwise, check with an SBA state field office or a Small Business Development Center—look in phone directories.

The *Management Aids* series are brief (less than 10 pages) discussions of approaches to making specific decisions. They cover a wide range of topics such as "Setting Pay for Government Management Jobs" (MA No. 195) and "Selling Products on Consignment" (MA No. 230).

The *Small Marketers Aids* series is a similar service dealing with specific topics germane to retail and wholesale operations.

The *Small Business Bibliography* series provides data sources, books, and article citations useful in investigating specific business opportunities. Many cover a single business such as "Restaurants and Catering" (SBB No. 17), although some do address generic functional areas (e.g., "Buying for Retail Stores" SBB No. 37).

The *Small Business Management* series consists of far more detailed treatments of management topics. These are in paperback book form and, again, cover a multitude of topics (e.g., "Small Store Planning for Growth" SBMS No. 33).

Ordering information and lists of series titles can be obtained from the SBA field offices. With the exception of the

Small Business Management series all publications are free. Nominal fees are charged for the SBM series.

Miscellaneous

Franchise Opportunities Handbook (Government Documents of Reference Section)   Published by the Department of Commerce. Contains brief descriptions of franchise operators, including addresses, number of franchisees, capital requirements, training and managerial assistance provided.

COMMERCIAL SERVICES

Market Data

Survey of Buying Power (Business or Reference Section)

> Sales Management, Inc.
> 630 Third Avenue
> New York, NY 10017

An updating and reformating of a variety of census and other data. Designed specifically for business applications, including determining market potential.

Comparative Ratio and Operating Characteristics

Financial Studies of the Small Business (Business or Reference Section)

> Financial Research Associates
> 340 W. Central Ave., Suite 210
> P.O. Box 2502
> Winter Haven, Florida 33883

Almanac of Business and Industrial Financial Ratios
(Business or Reference Section)

Leo Troy (Englewood Cliffs: Prentice-Hall)

Annual Statement Studies (Business or Reference Section)

Robert Morris Associates
Credit Division
Philadelphia National Bank Bldg.
Philadelphia, PA 19107

Small Business Reporter

Bank of America
P.O. Box 37000
San Francisco, CA 94134

Expenses in Retail Business

National Cash Register, Inc.

Inquire at your local NCR office. Request SP #1652. (The cost is $7.50.)

Market and Industry Studies

Predicasts 200 University Circle Research Center
11001 Cedar Ave.
Cleveland, Ohio 44106

Frost and Sullivan, Inc.
106 Fulton Street
New York, NY 10038

Industry Surveys   (Business or Reference Section)

Standard and Poor's Corp.
25 Broadway
New York, NY 10004

In depth analysis of 69 major domestic industries. Stock analyst opinions and future prospects. Good for identification of major trends, threats, and the major participants in the industry.

TRADE ASSOCIATIONS

Directories of Associations

Encyclopedia of Associations (Reference Section)

Gale Research Company
2200 Book Tower
Detroit, Michigan 48226

National Trade and Professional Associations of the United States (Reference Section)

734 15th Street NW, Suite 601
Washington, D.C. 20005

Both of these directories list associations, their addresses, offices, and the number of members and give some indications of the materials available.

Franchises

International Franchise Association
1025 Corin Ave.
NW Washington, D.C. 20036

INDEX SERVICES (Reference Section)

The index services track the publications in various trade and business publications and organize them by topical coverage or industry. They are valuable tools for identifying articles that have been published in a wide array of journals and magazines:

> *Business Periodicals Index*
> *Funk and Scott's Index of Corporations and Industries*
> *Wall Street Journal Index* (annotated)
> *New York Times Index* (annotated)

The latter two services compile only articles that have appeared in their respective newspapers.

Appendix B

Some Selected Readings for Extension and Future Development

We've relied on nontechnical forecasting approaches and the use of existing (secondary) market data. The next step in your development as a forecaster involves understanding of (1) statistical forecasting techniques—those we classified as data-based in Chapter 2—and (2) primary data collection techniques such as survey design and sampling.

The following books are intended to provide an introductory foundation for your continued development as a forecaster.

Statistical Approaches to Forecasting

The Beginning Forecaster: The Forecasting Process through Data Analysis, by M. Levenback and J. Cleary (Belmont, Cal.: Lifetime Learning Publications, 1981).

Regression Analysis by Example, by S. Chatterjee and B. Price (New York: John Wiley and Sons, 1977).

An Executive's Guide to Forecasting, by J. Chambers, S. Mullick, and D. Smith (New York: John Wiley and Sons, 1974).

Fundamentals of Forecasting, by W. Sullivan and W. Claycombe (Reston, Va.: Reston Publishing Co., 1977).

Marketing Research

Do-It-Yourself Marketing Research, 2nd Ed., by G. Breen and A. Blankenship (New York: McGraw-Hill, 1982).

Complete Handbook of Profitable Marketing Research Techniques, by R. Vichas (Englewood Cliffs, N.J.: Prentice-Hall, 1982).

Marketing Research, 5th Ed., by D. Luck, H. Wales, D. Taylor, and R. Rubin (Englewood Cliffs, N.J.: Prentice-Hall, 1982).

Industrial Marketing Research, by D. Lee (New York: Van Nostrand Reinhold, 1984).

Marketing Research, by F. Brown (Reading, Mass.: Addison-Wesley, 1980).

Appendix C

Personal Computer Spreadsheet Packages

The proliferation of personal computers has been accompanied by a dramatic increase in software packages available for small business operators. One of the most useful applications for the types of financial projections we've discussed is known generically as the "electronic spreadsheet." The programs permit the user to develop projected profit-and-loss and cash-flow statements, apply various growth percentages to sales and expense items, perform breakeven analysis, and do other manipulations. Of course, it's nothing you can't do with a pad and a calculator. However, the ease, speed, and accuracy of these programs encourage the user to ask "what if?" types of questions. For example, "What if sales increase by 5 percent per month instead of 8 percent?"; "What if variable costs exceed the forecast by 3 percent?"; "What if interest rates rise 2 percentage points over the first year?"

Answering such questions by hand is tedious, but a snap with a spreadsheet program. Because these products are changing and developing so rapidly, your best source of information is a retail computer dealer in your area. The retailers carry various packages, maintain libraries of books on their use, and offer tutorials and demonstrations. Many of the popular packages also offer more than just spreadsheet capabilities. It is common to get graphic capabilities, word processing, and database management functions in these packages. Some of the currently popular packages and a sampling of books and their use are listed below.

Currently Popular Packages

Lotus 1-2-3 and Symphony—Lotus Corp.

Framework—Ashton-Tate Corp.

VisiCalc—Visicorp.

SuperCalc—Software Arts, Inc.

Multiplan—Microsoft Corp.

PSS-Plan—Software Publishing Co.

Books

The Power of: VisiCalc, by R. E. Williams, B. J. Taylor, and B. L. King (Portland, OR: Management Information Source, 1983).

The Power of: SuperCalc, by R. E. Williams and B. J. Taylor (Portland, OR: Management Information Source, 1983).

The Power of: Multiplan, by R. E. Williams (Portland, OR: Management Information Source, 1982).

The Power of: Lotus 1-2-3, by R. E. Williams (Portland, OR: Management Information Source, 1983).

1-2-3 for Business, by H. McLaughlin and L. Anderson (Indianapolis: Que Corp., 1984).

All about 1-2-3, by R. Schware and A. Trembour (Beoveston, OR: Dilithium Press, 1983).

SuperCalc Super Models for Business, by D. F. Cobb and G. B. Cobb (Indianapolis: Que Corp., 1983).

An Introduction to VisiCalc Matrixing for Apple and IBM, by H. Anbarlian (New York: McGraw-Hill, 1982). .PA

Appendix D

Sales Forecasting Techniques

DATA-BASED TECHNIQUES

Each data-based technique has as its objective the quantitative definition of the relationship between sales and some other variable or set of variables. The statistical procedures used can be confusing, and if used improperly, the results of the analysis can be biased. Nonetheless, if reliable data are available, these techniques can provide valuable predictions of sales activity.

Correlation Analysis

A correlation coefficient is a measure of the degree of association between two series of data. In our applications of correlational analysis, one of the series would be a measure of sales, the other some measure of a variable we believe to vary with sales levels.

The correlation coefficient can range from -1 to $+1$. A correlation coefficient of zero indicates that the two series are unrelated. That is, they change independently of one another. The closer the correlation coefficient is to $+1$, the more the two series move in tandem; as one increases or decreases, the other does likewise. To illustrate a positive correlation, examine the data in Figure D-1, from a supermarket chain. The executives expect a positive correlation between average monthly store revenue and the number of households in the trade area.

Store #	Households (thousands)	Average Monthly Sales Revenue (thousands)
1	79	569
2	23	121
3	50	474
4	32	488
5	72	1,796
6	26	200
7	29	386
8	28	207
9	22	533
10	30	727
11	37	460
12	24	569
13	81	1,491
14	49	514
15	38	517
16	32	295
17	24	242
18	53	1,418
19	31	639
20	39	592
21	63	802
22	76	914
23	30	291
24	27	237
25	43	299

FIGURE D-1 SUPERMARKET CHAIN DATA

As they expected, number of households and monthly revenue are correlated. The correlation coefficient is + 0.71, indicating a strong positive association between the two variables.

A negative correlation coefficient results from data series that move in opposite directions. County unemployment rates and new car sales are likely to be negatively correlated.

In order to be of value in forecasting, correlation analyses must meet several conditions:

1. Coefficients should be near – 1 or + 1, indicating a strong degree of association.

2. The correlation should depict a stable relationship. If the relationship between the variables has changed since the data series were constructed, the value of correlation analysis is questionable.

3. The sales correlate (e.g., number of households, per capita income) must be predictable. If we can't estimate the future value of the sales correlate, little has been gained through the analysis.

Regression Analysis

Regression is the most widely used tool for quantifying relationships among variables. The relationship between a dependent variable (usually sales) and one or more independent variables can be mathematically defined. Consider the supermarket data again. Pleased to know such a strong relationship exists between households and sales, the executives are interested in knowing the exact form of this relationship.

By plotting the 25 stores on a graph, the correlation becomes apparent. In fact, one could "eyeball" a line like the dotted line in Exhibit D-1 through the data points. The line seems to represent the trend in the data fairly.

Regression analysis is a method of determining the mathematical definition of a line that meets certain criteria.

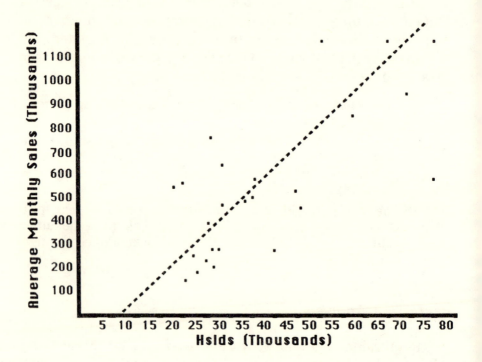

EXHIBIT D-1   SUPERMARKET CHAIN DATA

The most common criterion is called *least squares*. With the least squares criterion, the line chosen is the one that minimizes the sum of the squared deviations from each data point to the line.

The general formula for a linear relationship is

$y = a + bx$
where y is a dependent variable
    a is a y-axis intercept
    b is a regression coefficient
    x is an independent variable

Ordinary least squares was applied to the supermarket chain data, and the formula for the line was determined to be

y		a		b	x
Average Monthly Sales Revenue	=	-68.9	+	15.8	(thousands)

The formula implies that an increase of 1000 households to a trade area translates into $15,800 average monthly sales revenue. Armed with this information the executives can

- Forecast sales based on the estimated growth in trade areas they now serve
- Forecast store sales in new trade areas when additional stores are opened

Many forecasting problems are too complex for this simple linear approach involving only one independent variable. Multiple regression involves two or more independent variables. While more difficult to visualize, multiple regression does basically the same thing that simple linear regression did. The outcome is the definition of a *plane* that minimizes the sum of the squared deviations from the data points.

The specification of additional independent variables can improve forecast accuracy. In the supermarket example, variation in trade area households accounted for about 50 percent of the variation in average monthly sales revenue. The more variation we could explain, the better the model and in all probability the more accurate the forecasts we could generate.

Common sense tells us that factors other than the number of households influence supermarket sales revenue as well.

Household income, proportion of households with children, and number of competitors in the trade area are several variables that may be operating. Multiple regression could allow these variables to be incorporated into the analysis. Such a formula would have the following form:

$$y = a + b_1x_1 + b_2x_2 + b_3x_3 + b_4x_4$$

where y = average monthly sales revenue
a = y-axis intercept
x_1 = number of households
x_2 = average household income
x_3 = percentage of households with children under 18
x_4 = number of competitive supermarkets in the trade area
b_1, b_2, b_3, b_4 = regression coefficients

The multiple regression model is more typical of regression forecasting problems. Once the regression coefficients and the y-axis intercept have been estimated from historical data, future values of the independent variables can be entered to compute a forecast value for the dependent variable.

Time Series Analysis

A time series is the repeated measurement of a variable at intervals of time. Monthly sales figures for a company, the U.S. population, and the Dow Jones Industrial Average are all reported as time series. The assumption that underlies time series analysis is that historical values of a variable are meaningful for future predictions. In business situations, this assumption is not unreasonable. Structural changes in markets, however—new competitors, substitute goods, or new technology—could alter the value of historical observations for forecasting.

Time series analysis incorporates a family of techniques aimed at isolating sources—"components"—of variation in the series so that the effect on the forecast variable can be determined. In any time series the components of variations in data fall into four categories:

1. Long-term trends: an overall tendency for the data to increase, decrease, or remain constant

2. Seasonal variation: regular, periodic changes that recur in the data every year

3. Cyclical variation: patterns of expansion and contraction that repeat over a period longer than a year

4. Erratic variation: random changes caused by isolated, unpredictable events

Historical data can be used to estimate the effect of each component and reflect the components in the forecast. Specific procedures of time series analysis are well beyond the scope of this book, but its general procedure may be outlined:

Step 1: Develop seasonal adjustments through ratio-to-moving-average technique

Step 2: Estimate long-term trend through regression analysis of deseasonalized data

Step 3: Estimate erratic components through moving average or exponential smoothing techniques

Step 4: Develop cyclical adjustments

Step 5: Forecast future period with trend regression and apply seasonal and cyclical adjustments for final forecast

Each procedure for developing forecasts has its own advantages and disadvantages that require the forecaster to make trade-off decisions. The books listed in Appendix B introduce the reader these techniques, their characteristics, and their applications.

Input-Output Analysis and Econometric Models

These methodologies are best suited to larger businesses. They require:

1. Sophisticated statistical skills
2. A substantial pool of data
3. An understanding of the relationships among different levels and sectors of economic activity

Input-output methods have been employed successfully in economic development forecasts: for example, predicting the effects of a new plant location on a community. The *input* of investment capital and payroll can have several rounds of economic effects by stimulating retail and supply industries, which creates employment in those firms. Retail and supply payrolls and profits are also spent and saved, creating subsequent economic benefits. The input-output analysis technique attempts to capture those effects and predict *outputs* from the new inputs to the economic system.

Perhaps the best-known econometric models are those used for major sectors of the U.S. economy, maintained at economic consulting firms and government agencies. The models are complex, involving systems of equations that forecast various indicators of economic activity.

As our understanding of relationships between different forms of economic activity develops, the value of these forecasting methods will improve greatly.

JUDGMENTAL TECHNIQUES

As a group, judgmental techniques are intuitive approaches that blend experience and judgment. Most judgmental techniques are really "averages" of different opinions.

Sales Force Estimates

The proximity of salespeople to the customer and their intimate knowledge of the purchase decision make them an ideal source of forecast information. All members of the sales force are asked to make an educated estimate of sales in their respective territories for some future time period. The estimate can be formulated for individual products or product lines, by type of customer, and/or by new versus existing accounts. Aggregation of individual estimates from all salespeople is the basis of the sales forecast. Because this technique is inexpensive it can be employed as a check on the accuracy of forecasts developed by other methods.

Executive Consensus

A panel of executives from various functional areas of the company can offer the same blend of experience and judgment as the sales force. Marketing, finance, and production executives are generally included on the panel. Because the activities of their respective units will be affected by the forecast level of sales, they have clear ideas about the future. The panel format is the vehicle for arriving at a consensus of the executives' opinions.

Industry Expert Estimates

Consultants, market researchers, industry analysts, and trade association representatives can be called on. Their consensus theoretically represents a broader, more disinterested perspective than that of executives within the company.

Delphi Method

The Delphi method can be used to develop a consensus of either inside or outside experts. The participants need not know each other. The technique relies on several rounds of anonymous estimates, each followed by feedback to the participants on the consensus of each round. The feedback forms the basis of each participant's estimate in the next round.

Their forecasts, with supporting rationale, are transmitted to a coordinator. The coordinator forms a consensus forecast and a supporting summary rationale, providing it in writing to each participant. Participants respond with a new forecast and rationale. After several rounds of estimates, the forecasts should converge.

The technique is intended to bring the expertise of a number of people to bear on the forecasting problem without the dysfunctional aspects of group decision making. (Typical dysfunctions in groups include: the dominant personality, withdrawn participants, and conflicts among members.)

Historical Analogy

Often used in new product forecasting, historical analogy relies on knowledge of sales activity for a similar existing product or service in a similar market. Certain household appliances and consumer goods have demonstrated similar patterns of consumer acceptance and sales growth. The obvious difficulty is in identifying a product with similar appeal and target-market focus to use as a forecasting guide. In small firms, however, the sales history of existing facilities can be a valuable basis for forecasting sales of new sites or branch locations.

Intention-to-Buy Survey

The intention-to-buy survey, while similar to sales force and executive polling, is more direct in that it focuses on the intentions of the ultimate consumer. In consumer goods applications this technique usually samples potential customers. In industrial applications—where the number of customers may be small—sampling may not be necessary.

Purchase intentions can be difficult to obtain, and they are not always reliable. In practice, intention-to-buy surveys usually ask customers about

- The salience of product/service features
- Comparisons to existing substitute goods/services
- Relative price/quality tradeoffs
- The degree of satisfaction with existing products/services

Glossary

Glossary

Accounts receivable. Monies due from charge customers.

Advertising. Nonpersonal communications conducted through paid media.

Advertising agency. A firm that specializes in planning, preparing, and placing ads for clients with the media.

Aging schedule. A report showing how long accounts receivable have been outstanding. It gives the percent of receivables not past due and the percent past due by, for example, 30 days, 60 days, or other periods.

Amortization schedule. A schedule that shows precisely how a loan will be repaid. The schedule gives the required payment on each specific date and a breakdown of the payment showing how much of it constitutes interest and how much constitutes repayment of principal.

Amortize. To liquidate on an installment basis. An *amortized loan* is one in which the principal amount of the loan is repaid in installments during the life of the loan.

Anchor store(s). Principal tenant(s) of a shopping center.

Asset turnover. The ratio of sales to total assets available.

Balance sheet. An accounting statement that describes the financial condition of a business at a given time.

Benefit segmentation. Marketing approach that targets consumers according to the benefits they seek in a product.

Breakeven analysis. An analytical technique for studying the relation between fixed cost, variable cost, and profits. A *breakeven chart* graphically depicts the nature of breakeven analysis. The *breakeven point* represents the volume of sales at which total costs equal total revenues (that is, profits equal zero).

Budget. A plan of action expressed in figures.

Budget variance. The difference between the actual amount incurred and the budget figure.

Capital asset. An asset with a life of more than one year that is not bought and sold in the ordinary course of business.

Capital budgeting. The process of planning expenditures on assets whose returns are expected to extend beyond one year.

Capital intensity. The amount of assets required to finance each dollar of sales.

Capital structure. The percentage of each type of capital used by the firm: debt, preferred stock, and net worth. *Net worth* consists of capital, paid-in capital, and retained earnings.

Capitalization rate. A discount rate used to find the present value of a series of future cash receipts; sometimes called *discount rate.*

Carry-back; carry-forward. For income tax purposes, losses that can be carried backward or forward to other years to reduce federal income taxes.

Cash budget. A schedule showing cash flows (receipts, disbursements, and net cash) for a firm over a specified period.

Cash flow. The net effect of cash receipts and disbursements for a specified period.

Central business district (CBD). Downtown shopping area in the core of a city; usually the oldest shopping section in town.

Closely held corporation. A corporation that is not publicly owned; it is a corporation owned by a few individuals who are typically associated with the management of the firm. Also called a *closed corporation.*

Compensating balance. A required minimum checking account balance that a firm must maintain with a commercial bank. The required balance is generally equals 15 to 20 percent of the amount of loans outstanding. Compensating balances can raise the effective rate of interest on a loan.

Compound interest. An interest rate in which interest is calculated not only on the initial principal but also on the accumulated interest of prior periods.

Compounding. The arithmetic process of determining the final value of a payment or series of payments when compound interest is applied.

Consignment buying. A distribution arrangement in which a retailer acts as an agent for the supplier, taking title to and paying for only the merchandise sold.

Continuous budget. A budget that perpetually adds a month or a quarter in the future as the ending month or quarter is dropped.

Contribution margin. Excess of sales price over variable expenses. The amount of each sales dollar available to cover fixed expenses.

Convenience good. A good purchased with a minimum of effort, when the buyer has knowledge of product characteristics prior to shopping. Types are *staples, impulse,* and *emergency* goods.

Cost of capital. The rate of return on capital investment used in the budgeting process to set a goal for profitability.

Current assets. Assets that may be relied on or actively used for operating the business during the coming year.

Current liabilities. Debts that the organization must pay within the year following the balance sheet on which the current liabilities are listed.

Current ratio. A liquidity measure derived from balance-sheet information using the formula

Current ratio = Current assets ÷ Current liabilities

Delphi method. A modification of the *jury of executive opinion* in which executives' individually prepared estimates are reconsidered and a decision is made after a final round of refining.

Demographic segmentation. A marketing analysis that targets groups of prospects by factors such as sex, age, marital status, income, occupation, family size, and education.

Derived demand. The demand for industrial goods estimated on the basis of the demand for consumer goods. Manufacturers must be aware that they are selling through wholesalers and retailers, and not to the ultimate consumer.

Discounting. The process of finding the present value of a series of future cash flows. Discounting is the reverse of compounding.

Discounting of accounts receivable. Short-term financing arrangement in which accounts receivable are used to secure a loan. The lender does not buy the receivables, but simply uses them as collateral for the loan. Also called *pledging of accounts receivable.*

Discretionary income. Earnings remaining for luxuries after necessities are bought.

Disposable income. After-tax income available for spending and saving.

Factoring. A financing arrangement in which a firm sells its accounts receivable (generally without recourse) to a financial institution (the *factor*).

Fixed assets. Resources the firm will use over the years to come: buildings, vehicles, machinery, equipment, and so on.

Fixed charges. Costs that do not vary with the level of output, especially fixed financial costs such as interest, lease payments, and sinking fund payments.

Geographic segmentation. A marketing analysis that targets groups of prospects by geographic area.

Gross margin. For an item, the difference between its cost and its selling price; for a financial statement, an amount equal to the net sales during the accounting period less the direct (materials plus labor) cost of the goods sold.

Hurdle rate. In capital budgeting, the minimum acceptable rate of return on a project. If the expected rate of return is less than the hurdle rate, the project is not accepted. The hurdle rate should be equal to the marginal cost of capital.

Impulse goods. Items purchased on the impulse of a shopper who had not intended to buy.

Internal financing. Funds made available for capital budgeting and expansion of working capital through the normal operations of the firm. Internal financing is approximately equal to retained earnings plus depreciation.

Internal rate of return (IRR). The rate of return on an asset investment. The internal rate of return is calculated by finding the discount rate that equates the present value of future cash flows to the cost of the investment.

Jury of executive (or expert) opinion. A sales forecasting method in which the management of a company or other well-informed persons meet, discuss the future, and set sales estimates on the basis of their experience and intuition.

Lead time. The time elapsed between the placing of an order and the receipt of the goods ordered.

License plate analysis. A method of determining a retailer's trading area in which the residence addresses of vehicles parked near the retailer are found from vehicle registrations.

Lifestyle segmentation. A marketing analysis that targets groups of prospects by their activities, interests, and opinions.

Line of credit. A financing arrangement in which a lending institution (such as a bank or insurance company) commits itself to lend up to a certain amount during a specified period. The interest rate might not be specified in the agreement. A commitment fee is sometimes imposed on the borrower.

Manufacturers' representatives. Independent businesspeople or small firms that act as agents under contract for manufacturers.

Market segmentation. A marketing plan that targets a single well- defined group of consumers.

Meet-our-competition method. An advertising strategy that budgets an amount equal to the amount the competition is believed to be spending.

Mixed cost. A cost that has both fixed and variable elements.

Net present value (NPV) method. A method of ranking investment proposals. The NPV is equal to the present value of future returns, discounted at the marginal cost of capital, minus the present value of the cost of the investment.

Objective-and-task technique. An advertising strategy that begins with its promotional objectives and budgets an amount determined to satisfy those objectives.

Operating leverage. The extent to which fixed costs are used in a firm's operation. Breakeven analysis is used to measure the extent to which operating leverage is employed.

Payback period. The length of time required for the net revenues of an investment to return the cost of the investment.

Percentage-of-sales technique. An advertising strategy that budgets for promotion on the basis of a desired ratio of promotional expenditures to sales revenues.

Present value (PV). The value today of a future payment, or stream of payments, discounted at the appropriate discount rate.

Primary data. Original information that researchers gather firsthand.

Pro-forma statements. Forecasted financial statements.

Quick ratio. A measure of financial soundness: current assets minus inventory, divided by current liabilities. Sometimes called *acid test*.

Regression analysis. A statistical procedure for predicting the value of one variable (dependent variable) from knowledge of one or more other variables (independent variables).

Return on investment (rate of return). The most widely used single measure of a firm's operating efficiency. It equals either (1) the ratio of net income to invested capital or (2) asset turnover times margin on sales.

Run-of-paper (ROP). A newspaper advertising rate for ads whose placement the paper is free to decide.

Safety stock. A minimum inventory capable of meeting expected maximum demand and overcoming variations in lead time.

Sale and leaseback. An arrangement in which a firm sells land, buildings, or equipment to a financial institution and simultaneously executes an agreement to lease the property from the financial institution for a specified period under specified terms.

Sales force composite method. A sales forecasting method that derives predictions from surveys of sales representatives.

Secondary data. Data previously gathered for a purpose other than solving the problem under investigation.

Sensitivity analysis. Simulation analysis in which key variables are changed and the resulting change in the rate of return is observed.

Shopping good. A good whose product alternatives and product attributes must be investigated by consumers before they make a purchase decision.

Specialty good. A good for which consumers are brand loyal. Consumers are fully aware of the product's attributes before purchasing it, are willing to expend considerable effort to get the desired brand, and will pay a higher price for it than for competitors if necessary.

Standard Industrial Classification (SIC). A coding system for manufacturers, wholesalers, and retailers compiled by the U.S. Office of Management and Budget based on sales by product categories. Much data has been assembled for the SIC system.

Standard Metropolitan Statistical Area (SMSA). An integrated economic and social area with a large population and containing a central city with a minimum population of at least 50,000 (or two contiguous cities whose populations total 50,000).

Step-variable costs. Those variable costs that change abruptly at intervals because they involve large purchases that cannot be spread out over time.

Subchapter S. A section of the Internal Revenue Code that allows certain small business corporations to be taxed as either proprietorships or partnerships rather than as corporations.

Term loan. A loan with a maturity greater than one year. Term loans are generally amortized.

Time series extrapolation. A forecasting method in which historical sales data form the basis for projections into the future.

Traffic count. A tally of the number of people who pass a retail location at different times of day and on different days of the week.

Variable cost. A uniform per-unit cost that fluctuates in direct proportion to business volume.

Vendor. A supplier of component parts, supplies, or services to another organization.

What-we-can-afford method. An advertising strategy that budgets only surplus, after-profit, funds.

Working capital. A firm's investment in short-term assets: cash, short-term securities, accounts receivable, and inventories.

Index

Index

Accuracy, 10–11
Advertising budget, 80, 91
  methods for determining, 80–81
Anchor tenants, 55
ARBITRON, 69
Ashton-Tate Corporation, 144
Bank of America, 133
Breakeven analysis, 32–33, 86–87, 92–93
Cash flow, 36
Census data, 129–130
Central Bearings and Drives (illustration), 13–14
Competitive advantage, 34–35, 107–109
  sources of, 103–104
Competitors:
  analysis of, 101–102
Control cycle, 119–120
Continuous forecast, 124–125
Convenience goods, 52–53
Correlation analysis, 149–151
Cost-of-capital, 75, 93–95
Dark Room (illustration), 87–95, 106–113
Data-based forecasts, 21–22, 149–156

Delegation, 9
Depreciation expenses, 82–83
Differentiated products, 53
Delphi method, 157–158
Emergency Medical Center (illustration), 12–13, 26–37
Executive consensus, 157
Florists Transworld Delivery Association (FTD), 65, 68
F.I.C.A., 78–79
Financial Research Associates, 84, 132
Fixed asset requirements, 29–30, 76–77, 89
Fixed costs, 86–87, 91–92
Floral Supply (illustration), 65–69
Frost and Sullivan, 133
F.U.T.A., 78–79
Generative business, 55
Gale Research Company, 134
Historical analogy, 158
Industrial customer profile, 44–47
Industrial Supply (illustration), 12
Industry expert estimates, 157
Input-output analysis, 156
Intention-to-buy surveys, 158–159
Interest expenses, 82
International Franchise Association, 134
Judgemental forecasts, 22, 156–159
Locker Room (illustration), 56–59
Lotus Corporation, 144
Market potential, 27, 58–72
Market growth, 104–105
Market Potential–Sales Requirements approach, 3–4, 23–25
Marketing research, 140
Microsoft Corporation, 144
NAFEC, 26
Nonrecurring start-up expenses, 30, 77–78, 90
Operating expenses, 31–32, 78–83, 90
Payroll taxes, 78–79

Prodicasts, 133
Regression analysis, 151–154
Retail customer profile, 43–45
Robert Morris Associates, 133
Sales budgets, 31–32
  construction of, 85–95
Sales forecasting:
  benefits of, 14–17, 36–37
  relationship to planning, 15
  scenario development, 105–106, 110–112
  techniques, 21–23, 149–159
Sales force estimates, 157
Sales Management, Inc., 64, 132
Secondary data, 8
  examples of, 64, 68, 71, 84
  sources, 60–63, 85–85, 129–135
Shared business, 55
Shopping goods, 52
SMSA, 70
Software Arts, Inc., 144
Software Publishing Company, 144
Spreadsheet programs, 143–145
Standard and Poor's, 133
Statistical forecasting techniques, 139–140, 149–156
Suscipient business, 55
Target market, 26, 41–48
Time series analysis, 154–155
Trade area, 27, 51–55
  methods of defining, 55–56
Trade associations, 134
Variable costs, 86–87, 91–92, 122–124
Variance analysis, 120–124
Visicorp, 144
Volume adjustments, 120–121
WXXX-FM (illustration), 69–72